Master Li Chiao Fu - Wu Tang Chuan system - (see Chapter 9)

Esoteric Warriors

Alex Kozma

Paul H. Crompton Ltd.

FIRST EDITION 1999
REPRINTED 2001

Published by Paul H. Crompton Ltd.
London & New York

Gummerus Printing,
Jyväskylä, Finland 2001

ISBN: 1 874250 95 2

THE AUTHOR

Alex Kozma has practiced Buddhist and Taoist martial and meditation methods for fifteen years. In order to find genuine masters of these internal energy traditions he has travelled to the sacred mountains of the Himalayas and China, as well as to Taiwan, Hong Kong, Malaysia, North America and Europe. He continues travelling in the Far East to further his research.

THIS BOOK IS DEDICATED TO ALL THOSE

WHO MANIFEST WISDOM AND COMPASSION

IN OUR WORLD.

Contents

Acknowledgements

I had much support and help with this book. A big thank you to :

In the United Kingdom - Doug Ferar, Paul Whitrod, Sean Dervan (my first teacher),Fung Young (for making the China trip possible), Steven Benitez, Chris Chappel, Chris Demwell, Mike Gillespie, Shivanath and Gauri (for all the amazing retreats in Wales), Maha Kram, James Burn, Simon Das, James Oldham, Sebastian, Kakaia, and Pete Marsh for technical help; the Holland Park group - Trevor Jones (for his courage in training), Tony, Arnau, Francis (for Bagua inspiration), Roy, Jamie, Thomas, Ken Pang, Khan, Martin, Simon, Drummond, Robert, Kevin, Mike Donovan and of course Marcus Marriott; and the guys in Ashford, Colin, Rob, Jim, Danny, Leon, Roy, Speedy and Damon.. A special thank-you to Paul Crompton for believing in this project.

Thanks for love and inspiration from Maffo and Helena, my sister, and Anna, my mother, who kept the roof up when my head was in typewriter land. . . .

In France - Mark Baker (for sharing so much of the journey, over the years) and my teacher , Dr. Serge Augier.

In Taiwan - Chen Yun San, Eric Lo, Her Shun Ting, Shih Kuo Ping, Lin Huai-Mei and family (whose kind friendship made all the difference), Chen Mei Hua and Cindy Chen.

In China - Zhang Ya Kui and Mr. Zhang in O-Mei Shan, Master Li and students in Wu Tang Shan, and Ji Jian-Cheng, Wushu master of Hangchow University.

In Hong Kong - Lee Ah Loi, Leo Man (Pao Fa Lein Wing Chun), Master Ip Chee Kung and Grandmaster Ip Shui, David Hun, Deborah Hun, Tsang Tak Ning, Brian Sun, Sifu Chang in the New Territories, and Krsna Kanti.

In Penang, Malaysia - Cheong Cheng Leong and Ong Tat Ling.

In America - Bruce Kumar Frantzis and Bernard Langan, and Andy James.

A big thank you to Milan Kotecha of Gomark Graphics, with input from Suresh and Manoj. Jai Hanuman! And especially to Shervon Tham, for putting the packaging to one side for long enough to see the contents! And to Liz Paton for putting the whole thing together.

Publisher's Note

The Publishers wish to state that there are unusual martial arts methods described in this work.

The book is published only for descriptive purposes and is in no way meant to be a manual of instruction in whole or in part.

If you wish to train in any martial art or affiliated art you should seek the help of a qualified teacher.

Introduction

In recent years the internal martial arts have mushroomed in popularity in the West. Even the once obscure methods such as Hsing-I Chuan and Ba Gua Chang are now being taught by dozens of people in North America and Europe. Practitioners of these profound methods have discovered that they are much more than just superb fighting systems ; they can keep us healthy and active into old age, enable us to become aware of progressively more subtle levels of energy and consciousness, strengthen our minds, and let us access a place of stillness in the midst of the chaos and stress of modern-day living.

There are many purely technical books on the internal martial arts but few as yet that have given the broad perspective of many different masters and systems in one work. An exception, of course, is Robert W. Smith's excellent Chinese Boxing - Masters and Methods, which set many of us on the journey East. For the past ten years I have studied with and interviewed many skilled teachers of our generation, and recorded their teachings and ideas on the internal arts and how these practices relate to fighting, spirituality and meditation, healing, compassion and many other topics.

All of the teachers I spent time with were interesting characters in their own right, with unusually strong energy and a deep interest in spiritual practice. This work touches not only the Chinese systems, but also arts from Tibet and Indonesia. Most of the teachers are still actively teaching, and whether in Taiwan, Hong Kong, China, Malaysia or Europe, each went out of his way to share with me the arts and ideas which have given them a great sense of freedom and joy. It has been a privilege to record these teachings and relate them for you, the reader. My gratitude goes to every one of these teachers. It is my feeling that in future generations people will look back on some of them as being amongst the great masters of the time. My hope is that through this book their teachings can touch and inspire many more people around the world who are practising the internal martial arts, and help all of us to manifest more compassion and awareness in a society that is killing itself and it's home planet for lack of real spirituality.

Chapter One

Dr. Serge Augier - The Natural Boxer

One day I received a telephone call out of the blue from a man who had read some of my writing. In a strong French accent he claimed to be interested in learning the twelve animal forms of Hsing-I Chuan, saying that he had "done a little" Hsing-I practice.

Something in his voice caught my attention, and when we met the next day in a London park I could see at once from the man's eyes that he had done more than a little of something. We talked for a while before he showed me a form from the southern White Crane boxing system. The movements were extremely quick, loose and powerful and I knew at that moment that I would not be teaching him anything! For the next few months I studied with him almost every day for several hours on the roof of his apartment, and that was the beginning of a relationship which has grown stronger with the passing of time.

Serge Augier showing Ward Off Tai Chi movement.

A week after that first encounter I discovered that my new teacher had been training since he was nine years old, knew at least five different ways of doing each of the Hsing-I forms, and was the inheritor of the famed Tzuranmen or Natural Boxing system! If anyone I have met could be called a walking encyclopedia of martial arts it is this man, Dr. Serge Augier.

He has made nine trips to China to study internal boxing, including four periods of study with the renowned Grandmaster Wan Lai Shan of Tzuranmen. It was under Wan's direct guidance that he learned the old Ba Gua Chang style of Fire and Water Boxing. Later he studied under Su Dong Shen in Tokyo for two years, absorbing the Essence of Change style from one of that city's most respected fighters. Serge also went to

Serge Augier showing a Tzuranmen technique on author.

Taiwan, India, Indonesia, Brazil and Spain to study those countries' indigenous martial arts, and he lived in California for three years in the home of Bruce Lee's disciple Richard Bustillo to whom he still refers with great respect, as one of the most practical fighters he has ever met. A true researcher of martial arts no matter what their country of origin, he literally lives, breathes and sleeps the subject.

The times I lived with Serge, in his home in Paris, or in London and Wales, were full of the best kind of learning, which has no barriers or demands and which is a true exchange of energy, a real sharing. His grandmaster Wan Lai Shan once told him to learn from the young masters, since Wan said that he himself was most inspired in his twenties. He said that in our generation the best teachers would be young men. Serge himself is in his late twenties, and after studying with him and the other 'young masters' described in this book, I have to conclude that there was a lot of truth in Wan's statement.

Although he teaches in seminars around the world, Serge has only four close students, choosing to earn his living from practicing acupuncture. An extremely bright and funny man, his students learn as much from him over tea or a meal as they do during physical practice. His preferred teaching method is to live with his students for days or a week at a time, and at such times one is sucked into a martial arts vortex which seemingly rests only to eat or to sleep. What really comes through in these periods is the energy of his teachers, who are or were some of the 'heavyweights' (in skill terms) of Chinese boxing.

Alongside Wan Lai Shan and his disciple Huang Tian Xion, Serge studied intensely with Dr. Yang Jwing-Ming (the famed writer and chin-na expert), several mainland Chinese White Crane masters, and Su Dong Chen of Tokyo. Su, a bodyguard for various businessmen, is something

Serge Augier showing a Bagua (Pakua) application on author.

of a legend in his own lifetime. Once, when he was fourteen years old, he was thrown in jail in Taiwan for being drunk. His teacher, Hung I-Hsiang (whose name appears elsewhere in this book), had already arranged for him to fight at a tournament, so in the early hours of the morning Hung bailed Su out and took him to the fighting arena. Still drunk, Su fought against grown men and proceeded to win the contest.

Serge himself is a seasoned combatant, although maybe not through choice. Of medium build and with his youthful good looks, he appears to be anything but a fighter, although many have found out to their cost that a fighter he definitely is. Never boastful, he talks about his combat experiences in analytical and practical terms, always sounding regretful that people would see him as an easy target. His tactics always seem to start with "I saw him move slightly so I. . . . .", or "I am sure he started to hit me so I. . . . . "

What was interesting for me were the psychological changes I encountered during my training with Serge. I had always suppressed my anger and in fact during my entire life I had never once lost my temper. In retrospect, subconsciously I had considered it 'wrong' for someone 'walking a spiritual path' to get angry. How stupid I was! Of course, this seriously inhibited my ability to apply my martial techniques with real emotional content. Emotional energy is a stage that one has to pass through on the martial arts path, and I have yet to meet any master who has not done so.

There are many aspects to learning the martial arts, and this is one that my previous teachers had not dealt with yet. Maybe I had not been ready for that lesson before, but with Serge it was to come up very strongly. We had been doing a training retreat in the hills of Wales, along with another of his students. The first two days went well, and the energy built up with the intense practice of partner fighting drills and knife techniques. On the third day, training outdoors beneath the sunshine, Serge stepped up the pressure. He began to hit me, and only me, hard and often. I was used to that kind of pain from my years of training with such teachers. But now he continued relentlessly, almost (it felt to me) sadistically, slashing and cutting and hitting with a hard rubber knife so that I could feel the bruises coming up on my body. Behind the strikes was real aggression. I tried to defend myself, to fight back, but Serge advanced on me in such a way that I tied myself up. Whack!! I got hit across the body very hard, and in that moment it came roaring up out of the depths of my mind/body, a feeling of primal anger, a raw energy that was going to lash out and destroy. I knew that when Serge next came at me I would hit him as hard as I possibly could, teacher or not. And then he simply stopped. Smiling nicely at me he said, "End of lesson", and walked into the house. I stood there for a long time, the veins on my neck pumping with blood, my teeth clenched, breathing deeply, eyes glaring at the trees. I became aware of an energy, a great force, that I had never felt before. Anger? If this was anger. . . . why had I denied myself it for so long? Yes, anger is an energy. . . . . fear is an energy. . . . . why had I suppressed them so much when these emotions are natural energies? Of course, to take these energies out on other people is the opposite extreme, and one which can bring heavy karmic consequences. As always, the challenge for me was to find the balance. Lessons such as that one happen all the time with Serge, and serve to reinforce just how skilled and subtle a teacher he is. This is his story, in his own words.

Training With Master Huang And Grandmaster Wan Lai Shan

When I was nine years old my father employed a new cook for the family, a man from China named Huang Tian Xion. My father was one of the first Aikido black belts in France, so he must have felt a certain empathy with Huang who, I discovered, was the inheritor of an old Taoist martial art system called Tzuranmen. He was the disciple of the famed Grandmaster Wan Lai Shan, and was a political refugee escaping from China who somehow ended up in Paris. Both Huang and Wan had been guerrilla fighters in China and had spent time as political prisoners in that country's jails.

I had no choice as a nine year old kid, I had to learn the martial arts from Huang. Every morning and evening he would teach me. It was not very appealing since I had to wake up before everyone else! By the time I was fifteen I got a little bored with all the slow motion stuff, the sliding footwork and so on. My friends at the time were all doing karate, kickboxing or boxing, lots of fighting techniques and sparring. I really wanted to do that as well. My teacher said, "Fine, go and do karate, or whatever you like! "So for a while I went and did some of these things, though I was still training daily with him.

A big turning point came at an open Karate Championship in France which I entered. I found that I was unable to use my karate techniques, but each time my attacker was getting too good, or I was getting scared, my real teaching came out. I was excluded from the event but I was happy. My techniques were not approved of but they were working very well! Right then I realised how good Huang's teaching had been.

When I was seventeen I went to China with my teacher. I saw many different systems there that we never see in the Occident. Then I met Grandmaster Wan Lai Shan for the first time. Wan is famous throughout China for his abilities as a fighter. In his early twenties he wrote a martial art book which revealed many of the secrets of internal boxing and Taoist chi-gung, and for years afterwards masters would turn up on his doorstep and challenge him to fight, wondering how such a young man could dare to reveal such things! Wan never refused a challenge and by all accounts never lost a match, and eventually people stopped coming to fight him and he became a renowned teacher. In fact Wan was champion of the first all-China martial art championship in the early 1920's. He had many teachers. Originally he studied the Six Harmony Shaolin system with Chao Hung-Chou, but his main teacher was the almost legendary Du Xing Wu who passed on to Wan the Tzuranmen, or Natural Boxing system. Wan also studied the three main internal martial arts; as an example of his depth of research into these methods, he knew eighty different ways of doing the Single Palm Change of Ba Gua Chang!

Wan Lai Shan with Huang Tian Xian

In Tzuranmen we don't have forms. Rather we use little combinations of techniques, lots of energy work and two man drills, footwork exercises and various other methods. There are also all the esoteric methods such as the Taoist hypnotism and mind techniques. So on this first trip to China I started doing specific Ba Gua, Hsing-I, Tai Chi styles, along with the Tzuranmen concepts. The way I had learned from my teacher before this was interesting. He would give me maybe one Tzuranmen technique, a Ba Gua palm change, and some strength drills for me to work on, and that would be one lesson. Only much later, in my mid-twenties, did I really organise everything into a system that would be cohesive for teaching.

All of Tzuranmen is based on Taoist meditation. For the fighting idea you have key concepts. You will look at an opponent's body sectors or gates, and by the gates you will have two or three ways to enter. Each time you can do it in one motion, like defending and attacking simultaneously, or in two motions, like slap-parry-HIT! Then you go to three, four. . . . up to eight motions. You build up these quick combinations of hitting and kicking. Then you apply it with a partner to make it real.

That first meeting with Wan was an eye opener. He was sitting there watching his students training, and every time he went to get up every one would be scared. He was more than eighty five years old at the time, but still very strong and fierce. Each day he was running in the hills to keep fit. As I watched he took a nail between his two fingers and put it into a board with a whipping motion of his arm. He told me that this was the correct striking motion. Then he took a bag of herbs and hit it with his fingers. He said that it made the fingers strong without hurting them. I said, "Yes, yes?" and I didn't see what he was getting at until he went WHACK! and said, "This is the application!"I had the mark on me for two weeks!

Tzuranmen is a very difficult system to find. Up until Wan it was passed down from one master to one disciple. We know that a Taoist named Little Xu taught it to Du Xing Wu, after an encounter in which the extremely tall and skilled Du was toppled by the dwarf Xu. Du Xing Wu, who was famous for his light body chi gung and point-hitting skills amongst other things, taught only Wan Lai Shan, and Wan in turn taught Tzuranmen to only three disciples, my teacher Huang being the first one. The other two disciples, whom I met, vanished after Wan's death (in the early 1990's), but Wan also had many students who learned his Six Harmony Shaolin style

Tzuranmen is different each time you see it done, because the system wants you to be different. Your system will be completely different to the other practitioner, but you will share the same concepts. My teacher Huang has his apartment in Paris, and when I go to see him I still see a lot of Chinese people who have heard about him and come to ask if he will teach them the Tzuranmen system. He refuses, saying that he only teaches Tai Chi Chuan. He has always avoided fighting situations in France, although one time he nearly killed a guy who was hurting a lady. I was his only Tzuranmen student, because he lived with me and knew that we would have at least fifteen years together. Even now, at eighty five, he is very healthy. When he does his Tai Chi you will see that every part of his body is moving as one, nothing stops moving by itself.

One time my teacher was showing me sword. I was sixteen, and before that we had always used a piece of stick to train sword techniques with. So we were in the countryside and he had just given me a real sword. I was so happy to have it that I went around cutting herbs and grass, and I was in the field cutting everything I could find. I was whacked over the head so hard that I fell to the ground. I didn't know why I was hit. My teacher told me to hold the tree very low, which meant that he was angry. After a while I asked him why he had hit me, and he said, "How can you respect the art if you don't respect the weapon? "That was a good lesson

Not very long ago I went to see him in Paris. We had left a restaurant and we were walking home in the dark. A lady was being bothered by some guy, and my teacher said to walk in front of them to make sure she was okay. I'm sure he sensed that something was really wrong. When we caught up with them the man was slapping the lady over and over again, really wild. My teacher said very nicely to the guy to stop it. The man just started to curse my teacher. I'm not sure, but I think that the guy stepped towards him, and my teacher gave him this BIG slap on his head. The hit didn't push him away at all. He just fell right where he was, like a piece of clothing. It was so intense, one minute he was alive, the next he was out! The first thing I did was to take the guy's pulse. . . . . he was completely out. The lady was in shock, and by the time we had finished helping her twenty minutes had passed. Still the guy was unconscious. I left him there, completely out.

Training In The East And West

When I was nineteen I went to California, and I lived in the school of Richard Bustillo (who developed Jeet Kune Do concepts with Dan Inosanto.) Richard's fighting ability is excellent, but he keeps out of the spotlight. At his school you would find cops and gangsters training together since it was in one of L. A. 's rougher neighbourhoods, and the emphasis was on practical techniques that worked. I was this little French guy, new to the school, up against these huge Americans, and I had a good chance to see how my previous training would work against bigger attackers.

I got a job in a bar, guarding the door, and for the first two weeks I was quite happy with my techniques since I was able to beat everyone who was causing trouble no matter the difference in size. Then one night this guy came at me very quickly, and though I thought I had stopped him I still felt this pain in my stomach. I felt something wet and looking down I saw that I had been stabbed. It was a very deep wound and I was rushed to hospital. Afterwards I really had to rethink what I was practicing. Up until then I had been doing a lot of forms, all of the Hsing-I twelve animal sets and so on, for quite a while. I was really into that, but after the stabbing I stopped that and returned to intensive training for reactions and power

From California I was lucky enough to travel to Indonesia and the Phillipines, and I learned from different masters in Kali and Pentjak Silat. I stayed at a silat school where the training included having to face being ambushed by multiple armed attackers in the jungle! The systems out there have excellent techniques and flow, and when I returned to the States I met and trained with many masters of Silat and Kun Tao. The Silat styles are very much based on concepts, and in Indonesia I saw several systems which are very close to Ba Gua. . . . they turn and spin and move around. . . . and that changed the way I saw Ba Gua.

After that I returned to France and went in the army, and there I was able to practice my fighting a lot! In the French army you are there because you have to be there, not by choice, so people are very tense and there are fights every day.

After the army I continued to study acupuncture and medicine, in America, Paris and China. I met Dr. Yang Jwing-Ming of Boston, who didn't teach me specific styles exactly but over the last eight years or so he has given me a lot in the way of chin-na and other things. His speciality is White-Crane Boxing. He is a real master in the true sense of the word, mature, skilled and with a deep knowledge. His books are great. If you talk to him about technique he will talk concept. If you talk concept he will talk religion. If you talk religion he will talk philosophy.

The thing that completely changed my way of seeing the internal martial arts was meeting Su Dong Chen of Japan. From the applications which were a little too intricate, and took too much time, Su had this way to use any part of the Ba Gua or Hsing-I or Tai Chi, and to make it into a boxing-moving system with throwing and locking that really worked. He is the most amazing fighter I have seen anywhere, China, America, Europe, and he has the power of someone three times my size. His power is not normal for his size. Each time he touches you, with his finger, his leg, his head, it is not hurting you in the normal way. He is amazing, but he really is in the fighting way, he is a real warrior and is not too much into the chi gung health aspect. He goes more for the short intense life. If he was to meet the Tao he would kick it's butt! He knows weapons techniques but doesn't teach them, because he says as soon as you pick up a weapon you are not a real warrior. His arm, from beginning of fingers, to the elbows, is like a puzzle of scars where he has been cut so many times. You can see he is good because the cuts stop at the elbow, and the only cuts and bullet scars he has on his body are on the side so you know that he was turning. He is excellent at fighting. His attitude towards fear is that you should confront it directly. Once I was training in the park with a knife and he came to see me. He told me that he wasn't afraid of knives and showed me why. He took the weapon from me, and it was sharp, and without any hesitation he cut his arm before giving it back to me! That was why he wasn't afraid of blades!

All of the tricks he gave me, and all the long conversations we had, mostly in bars and restaurants, really changed my vision of the internal arts. Su had learned from the Hung family in Taiwan before travelling and training with many people. The big change in his life was meeting the famous Shwai Chiao (Chinese Wrestling) master Chang Dung-Sheng, the creator of the Chang Tai Chi style. This was a big revelation for Su, and what he does now is not even called Ba Gua or Hsing-I since it is too different from these styles. He calls it Essence of Change, and teaches some students in Tokyo.

Another time I saw Su demonstrating short-power hitting, striking without range. He showed it on this striking board, and everyone was so used to seeing him perform that they were just going like, "Oh yeah, very nice! "Well, Su got a little angry, and he breathed deeply once or twice really hard and the hair stood up on his arms. His chi is so strong that he can make the hair stand up at will. He hit the striking board which was being held by this man. The guy took a step back and you could see that he was bleeding. I was wondering how the strike could cut the skin through a board, but no, the strike was so hard that it broke the wood, and the wood cut the surface of the man's skin. That was a real display of Fa Jing (explosive power)!

On Internal And External Training

Martial arts to me is about living a long time in perfect health, so that you don't have to limp around for the last twenty years of your life. I would say that any system is good if it doesn't damage your body in the long run..

The external martial arts start from muscular strength, they make the body very hard. If you want to live a long time, however, at some point you have to switch to internal methods. So normally they go from hard to soft. Many of them stay at the hard stage because it feels so powerful. This is why in China many teachers who do a lot of hard chi-gung and hard practices die of energy-dispersion in their middle age. It is called energy-dispersion because you build up a lot of energy and power in your youth and then one day, OOPS!, you get a little sick, maybe a cold or fever, and you have to stay in bed. Then very quickly, over a few days or weeks, you start getting cancers, or organs going wrong, and then you die very quickly. This is because you have built up too much tension and you cannot maintain it. It is really bad, and it happens to many good practitioners.

The internal martial arts, on the other hand, will start very softly, doing soft and dance-like things in the beginning to build the chi. After, when they have built up their chi, they go slowly to hard. When you have developed softness, flexibility, whipping, good combinations and so on, then you can start to hit hard and make your body hard, because already chi is flowing through you. Then you can do the hard practices, but it takes longer this way. But at least you can live much longer. In hard styles you go from the other side, and most of the time you get stuck there because you feel powerful. . . . . but you are not, your chi is dead.

Then you see something like White-Crane, which is in the middle. You are already soft and hard at the same time. The problem is that if you emit fa-jing without making your body strong then the vibration will slowly tear your tendons and muscles and organs. You can mess up your spinal cord, knees and joints. It is fine if you are strong naturally or if you train to make your body strong. Because of the twisting movements in White-Crane, and the way you emit power, you can damage your organs. You have to train with a good master who will explain how your body works. Then you know that you need to make your muscle and tendon strong before you can do the twisting and the whipping movements. In White-Crane they hold the postures not just to memorise them, but to harden the tendons also. White-Crane has always been the system that has given masters of other styles the biggest problems. Even the founder of I-Chuan (Mind Boxing), the famous Wang Hsiang-Chai, was undefeated until a White-Crane master beat him. All of these systems from south China like White-Crane, southern Mantis and Bak Mei (White Eyebrow), are very practical fighting methods which develop great striking power, but they do have health risks inherent in the training.

At the beginning of training the internal arts you will cultivate the chi for a free flow of energy. You do standing exercises like Holding the Tree, that will just make you aware of your chi. When you become aware of what it is, of the feeling, then you can start to find it when you move. For example, in Tai Chi you are told to direct your chi to certain points. Great! But if you don't know what this energy is, how can you direct it? So first you must find it. In Holding the Tree, if you stand still long enough and then release the posture, you will know what chi is! Then after, in your form, it is easy to find it.

Next you can build up the chi by abdominal breathing and small circulation, and then once you have something to emit you can begin doing fa-jing (explosive power) using the whipping motion. It is a very progressive system which takes time.

For a long time your teacher will tell you, "Relax, it will come one day", and you will say "Sure, sure!", and only do it because if you don't you get whacked over the head! That was my case! But one day you are training and "Wow!", something really happens. I was always very skinny and small and people were always challenging me to fight. For a long time I would hit and kick and nothing really worked too well, but then one day. . . . . it really worked! Then I found I was getting more impact the more relaxed I became, and then I put less power and more whipping motion and my fa-jing was really increasing. The key to fa-jing is this abdominal wave motion, along with mixing your chi inside, and then you will have something substantial to emit.

On Hsing-I, Tai Chi Chuan And Ba Gua

For each of the three systems you have three levels of practice. Tai Chi is the complete exercise of the consciousness. . . . the consciousness of the chi and the total body movement. When you do Tai Chi, everything moves together. Tai Chi is not HIT!. . . it's hit/move, hit/move.

Next is Ba Gua, which is the wave or whipping energy. A wave will crush, and then go back again. You hit and then whack!, then move, then hit again. . . . it's like water, soft and hard.

Hsing-I is the total body exercise, and it looks for the one big HIT! with the whole body. That is it's idea, to crush with one strike. . . . whereas Tai Chi will use more tearing and hitting, parrying and striking at the same time in a boxing style fashion. Of course you have the classic Tai Chi concepts of peng, li, ji and an, but after this you have separating, splitting, grabbing - all of the chin-na and throwing - and the ideas of hitting you and then bumping into you and then using elbows. It is very much the multiple attack, where I will hit you ten thousand times very fast. But Hsing-I will advance onto you and put you in such an awkward position that you can not defend against the one big punch that is coming. I will parry and enter and then strike. Hsing-I was taught to the army, it is very direct. . . . . . parry-step-HIT! and it is over!

Each Hsing-I movement is a very clearly experienced energy. Pi-Chuan, or splitting fist, is like throwing something. Tsuan Chuan. or drilling fist, is like jumping rope or skipping, because you have all the twisting motions, the spirals. So from these five energies you create your own techniques. It is very simple, yet very profound. Ba Gua for fighting has a little of everything. You can use boxing methods, grappling, throwing. . . . Ba Gua people tend to put whatever they know and specialise in into the applications. But the real speciality of Ba Gua is the way of using the palm to strike with no distance between the hand and the object being hit. The methods of developing this fa-jing in Ba Gua are very clear and effective.

Physically Hsing-I is easier to do than Tai Chi, because in Tai Chi everything must move together. In Ba Gua it is even harder because you have to turn all the time. But that is just the physical aspect. It is like talking about dancing. If you have time and you work hard, you will get it. But the essence of each style is very much harder to grasp. Hsing-I is the hardest because you don't have many techniques to play with. A good Hsing-I is more difficult to master than even a medium Ba Gua. For fighting, most of the time you will use the same movements because they are simple, fast, effective and powerful. In Hsing-I you will not find many people who are no good at fighting, because it's so simple. In the internal arts, the less you have flowery dancing type movements the more you can concentrate on the real thing. You have five motions which if you change them a little you get the applications. If you change them even more you have the twelve animals, and these give variety of usage to someone who is not so experienced in other systems. It is so simple. If you practice every day it goes out like a sneeze, like a natural reaction, you don't have to think about it.

With each system you have three main ideas - you can go against the force, with the force, or totally blend with the force. All martial arts are equally effective if they are practiced by someone who really wants to do something! Boxers from every system have been beaten at some point - so there is no one best fighting art. For example, Dong Hai Chuan was the best boxer of his era, but he could have been doing any style and still been the best! For me the system is good if it takes you a long way in perfect health.

On Taoism

Everything I know about Taoism is from Master Huang. There is a progression we follow which is the eight big steps to enlightenment. . . . and then beyond. When you have reached the nothingness you crush the nothingness! It is a long, long process, and living in a city or travelling around it is not possible to achieve the last steps. These are too difficult, they must be done alone, completely away from society and distractions.

Taoism and internal martial arts are both about balance, inner and outer balance. First you must regulate the body, then you can regulate the breathing and then the mind. It is a step by step method which is very clearly defined in the Tzuranmen tradition. I will give you an example of balance in Tai Chi which is often overlooked. In the form it is not good if you are always emitting power with fa-jing. . . . but at the same time it is bad if you never emit power. My teacher said it is like eating all the time without going to the toilet! So you must find the balance. Of course, it is different for each individual, and changes with age. For your chi to be of a good quality it must also be balanced, so your form must be done left and right sides, slow and fast.

I have been to China nine times, and each time I stayed a couple of months. You can see some strange things there. In Taiwan I met one hermit who was killing dogs by putting his two fingers inside them. In South China I saw a monk who was hitting wood with his palm and leaving the trace of his hand on the wood. His method was completely internal, using the power of the mind, without any external movement. This was the real I-Chuan or boxing of intention.

There are also systems in China which use singing and names and mantras, along with certain gestures of the hands. There are lines of motion which can disturb the mind of the attacker, and this can be very useful in fighting. We have these ideas and methods in Tzuranmen..

Maybe when I am fifty years old I will go and live in the mountains and complete the final stages of Taoist practice, but for now I am happy to live in the world and gather information. One lesson that always stands out comes from when I was a little younger. My teacher wanted me to have more intention in my fighting techniques, and he asked me if I knew the difference between eggs and bacon. I just shook my head. He said, "The chicken has some involvement with the eggs. The pig is committed to making the bacon!"

That is a question I would ask my student: are you just involved in this practice, or are you committed?

General Li's Tai Chi Chuan

The General Li Tai Chi Boxing taught by Serge Augier is the most complete Tai Chi system I have encountered, and it is worth taking a brief look at it's syllabus. Although a long form is practiced at a later stage, much of the emphasis in the first few years is put on the 'thirteen postures form', which, as the name suggests, comprises the thirteen essential energies of Tai Chi. This form has four very distinct stages.

1st stage - the form is repeated an equal number of times each side (most Tai Chi styles I have seen perform only one side of the form], and is done either very slowly, very fast, or a combination of the two. At this stage the student will also practice specific fa-jing drills, standing meditation, footwork drills and two man fighting sets which teach the practical usage of the form.

2nd stage - now each movement of the form is worked using big and small circles, and repeated hundreds of times by itself. The feeling at this stage is of the body becoming like a sphere, so that any force coming in is bounced away. This really works the energy of peng. A complete system of Taoist nei gung is practiced and built into the form

3rd stage - Now the form is transformed into a real boxing method, using dynamic footwork in all eight directions, multiple hand strikes to the vital-points using specific hand formations, and various ways of grabbing and tearing. Fighting against multiple attackers is taught

4th stage - The form becomes completely internalised, so that the various energies of Tai Chi are practiced inside the mind/body rather than as external movement. This stage will feed the first stage, and so the practitioner returns to the basic form but with all the energies wired into his system. In fighting one's applications are totally natural and spontaneous, and then one can go beyond the idea of fighting and use the energy for meditation and healing.

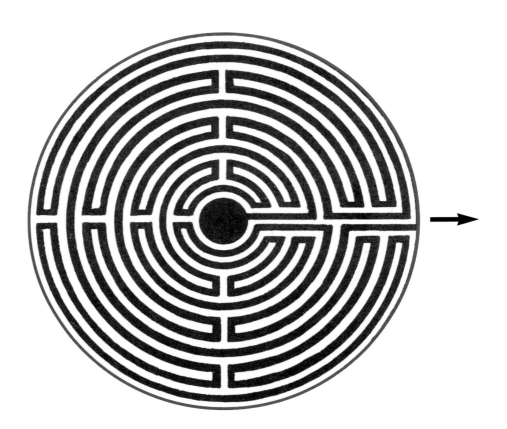

Chapter Two

Steven Benitez and Hasilkan Penuh Martial Arts

Picture the scene : a no-holds barred underground martial arts tournament held in England, attended mainly by Orientals with a smattering of Westerners. A youth, English-born but of Spanish descent, waits quietly on the sidelines for his final fight. Although still in his teens he has already won several of these tournaments using the punishing Chinese/Indonesian fighting art of Kun Tao. He is well prepared for a fight in which elbows, knees and head butts are permitted. The fight begins, but today something strange has happened to the youth. As his older and larger opponent rushes towards him he feels a joyous energy filling his mind and body, and instead of

Steve Benitez demonstrates.

closing his posture in the normal protective fashion he finds his arms and feet spontaneously opening up. It appears to him that the other man is moving in slow motion, like a leaf falling from a tree, and in that state he is able to effortlessly evade every punch and kick. Time after time it seems to those watching that the youth is hardly even moving or expending any energy, and yet the attacker cannot land a single blow.

Steve Benitez demonstrates his techiques on the author.

Then suddenly the youth explodes forward and the older man is thrown down and knocked out.

The fight is over. The youth has won yet another tournament, but this one is destined to change the direction of his entire martial arts career. He has no idea what has come over him, for instead of the aggression and adrenalin-fuelled rush of previous fights he now feels filled with bliss and compassion as his Kun Tao teacher and brothers congratulate him on his victory.

Ten years on Steven Benitez, the winner of that tournament, is a Christian pastor in London. I was fortunate enough to study with Steven over a five year period , and during that time he passed on to me the concepts and training methods of his unique Hasilkan Penuh system, which is an interesting blend of Kun-Tao, Silat and his own methods. I had been fascinated by the Indonesian arts for many years previous to that, for my first teacher, who studied in south east Asia, told me many stories about the wonderful skills attributed to the masters of Silat. One tale I always remembered concerned a middle-aged man, a worker at a rubber factory, who refused to give in to the demands of a group of thugs.

One night he was attacked, stabbed and beaten and left for dead. The next morning, however, the man turned up for work with not a mark on him. The gangsters, meanwhile, had developed various injuries during the night which somehow corresponded to the wounds on the workers body. One man died from a collapsed lung, another from a fractured skull, and so on. When asked by his fellow workers what he had done, the man said simply, "Silat!", and left the factory never to be seen again.

I met Steven in 1991 when he was selling incense from a flypitch in London's Covent Garden, and we connected as friends immediately. Strange things were happening to him at the time, for his subtle energies were awakening and he had no clear way of explaining them to himself. He had left the guidance of his first master who had told him that he needed to find a teacher who could guide him to the deepest levels of the martial arts.

Naturally friendly and open Steven agreed to show me what he had learned and what he had began to develop on his own. He began with Kun Tao, a blend of the most direct and brutal fighting techniques from Chinese boxing and Indonesian Silat. His speed was shocking. Then he showed some Harimau, or Tiger style, Pentjak Silat, crouching low to the ground before suddenly leaping in the air. He asked me to attack him as I wished, but the best of my strikes were met time after time with evasions and lightning-fast takedowns. He demonstrated how the various styles of Kun-Tao and Silat differed from one another, and then he showed the concepts and forms that he had developed himself. They were completely circular and spiralic in nature, very soft at times and then explosively quick, and the postures were alternately very low and then very upright. Steven's legs were like tree trunks, and he seemed to be completely at home on the ground.

When I asked who had taught him these methods he said that some of the knowledge had come to him in dreams and from intuition in his practice. The art still had a very Indonesian flavour, however. But still he was not satisfied. Ever since his heart-opening experience at the underground fighting tournament several years before, he had been trying to understand the link between the martial arts and spiritual practice. He had investigated various religions and meditation methods, but nothing had really touched his heart. So he had followed an age-old Indonesian ritual and fasted for seven days whilst praying for a teacher.

Ironically enough it was a few days after that fast that I met him and found in him a teacher and a good friend. He agreed to teach me his system, which was as yet unnamed, and thereafter we practiced in parks, temples, quiet courtyards and in our back gardens. Steven travelled to Holland and found a Pentjak Silat Maha-Guru (great master), a female mystic, who shared with him deeper aspects of the martial arts and spirituality. On his return his martial skills had obviously reached an even higher level, and many students joined his classes.. His martial art system had also been named by the Maha-Guru, who told Steven that his mission was to spread Pentjak Silat in the West : Hasilkan Penuh, an Indonesian term which translates as 'To produce Complete Martial Arts within Oneself', was the name that Steven called his unique system.

A school opened by Steven was full up on every night of training. But there was a great gulf in his heart. The more his students looked up to him with awe (and it was to be expected since Steven was manifesting some strange energies during the lessons) the more he was unable to align the feeling of compassion with the teaching of a brutal fighting system. He wanted to be in communion with God, and often during the lessons he would talk about Jesus Christ much to the bemusement of the trainees.

And then one day it happened. Steven had a profound mystical experience and gave his life to Christ. Slowly his teaching changed. The forms became a dance to God, a prayer, a communion. For the first time he felt at peace.

I have never seen more beautiful forms than those performed by Steven Benitez, and I am not sure I have ever met a fighter with as much speed and such perfect timing. The last time we met, just a week ago, he was working on another new method, something he calls the 'mystic wheel'. Seek him out if you can, but don't be suprised if he directs you to pray instead of teaching you his explosive martial art system!

What follows is his story, narrated by him in 1996.

"I began martial arts practice at the age of seven or eight. I learned Perrisai-Diri Silat and some Wing Chun with a couple of teachers, and then I met Jerry Tan, a Sumatran man who was to be my teacher for the next ten years. At first he taught me Northern Praying Mantis boxing, and then in my teens I learned his system of Kun-Tao, a very direct and vicious fighting method which involved the constant repetition of eight striking combinations both solo and with a partner.

We did a lot of practice to develop the fa jing, or shocking power, and a lot of full contact sparring whilst wearing crash-helmets which allowed head strikes. I also learned various methods of Pentjak Silat from Jerry and the masters who would often come and visit him. One such method was called Pocket, since it was the master's personal fighting technique which he kept to himself, or 'in his pocket'. Another was Running Silat, where you literally charge towards the opponent with multiple hand strikes. Then there is Broken Silat, which breaks down the forms and takes the most effective techniques and practices them with a partner for hours on end. At this stage of my life I was training six hours a day with my friends and by myself, and martial arts dominated my life. I learned Harimau Silat, which copies the spirit and actions of the Indonesian tiger, and would practice jumping high up in the air for long periods of time to develop my legs.

After my experience at the tournament where I had a big opening, many strange things began happening in my life. Myself and two of my martial arts brothers were training on Hampstead Heath when a terrible looking spirit appeared to us. We were terrified and ran through the forest, but there were ghosts hanging from the trees!I couldn't speak for days after that happened, and my friend completely changed. If one person sees such a thing it could be an illusion, but all three of us saw the same thing!

From this and other experiences I began to feel that a lot of martial artists were linking up with dark energies from which they drew their strength, either consciously or unconsciously. At that time I was desperate to find a teacher who could guide me through these strange things and help me understand what the martial arts meant. What I was really looking for was the Truth.

I went to different temples and religious groups, but in the end I just trained even harder to try and work out the answer. Jerry advised me to fast, so I did a seven day fast. I had planned to go to Indonesia after that and seek a Silat master, but the day that I broke the fast something strange happened. I met my friend Johnny, who was another senior student under Jerry Tan, and as we walked down the high street a beautiful looking woman, dressed entirely in white, stepped out in front of us and blocked our way. "The man you want is in there!" she said, and pointed to a cafe. We looked in the door and then looked back, but the woman had vanished into the crowd. We went inside the cafe, and saw a small, Indonesian-looking man seated alone at a table. He was staring directly at us with piercing eyes. Of course, we wondered if he was our new master! We introduced ourselves and asked him if he knew Pentjak Silat, and without saying anything he passed me a piece of paper and walked rapidly out of the cafe. We rushed after him but he weaved in and out of the crowds so quickly that within seconds we had lost him! I looked at the piece of paper. It said 'Harimau Bugat' and gave an address in a town in the north of Holland. Harimau Bugat was the feared Black Tiger style of Silat. We realised that the fasting had worked!

After saving our money for a while we travelled to Holland and took a train towards the north of the country. Half way through the journey the train stopped at a town, and without quite knowing why I told Johnny that we should jump out right there instead of going to our original destination. After a walking through the town someone told us of a woman who taught Pentjak Silat, and we went and knocked on her door. She was expecting us already! She led us into her front room, and it was full of strange carvings and paintings and Indonesian weapons. She was about fifty years old with powerful eyes. She spoke in a high-pitched sing-song voice, and told us not to put our hands over the red rope in the corner of the room. The rope protected an ornate looking Kris (Indonesian wavy-bladed knife) which sat on a purple cushion atop a table. The woman left and went upstairs, and being more than a little immature at the time we jokingly put our hands closer and closer to the red rope. The moment one of our hands crossed the rope the Kris swivelled on the cushion and we jumped back in shock!When the woman come back she told us off and said that the Kris didn't like to be approached by anyone but herself. The Indonesians are very superstitious about their weapons, believing that every blade has a spirit inside it.

Later we met some of the woman's students. We called her Ma, and found out that she had been born a Princess in a Javanese tribe but at the age of seven some holy men had come to her village and taken her to the mountains. There she underwent intense austerities for many years, until she manifested all of the mystical powers. Later she went to Holland and opened a school of martial arts, healing and spirituality. Her students consider her to be an Avatar, or one who has descended from a higher plane to guide mankind. I do know that she has some strange powers. Her way of doing martial arts was amazing. She was not slim, but she had a way of 'moving like a blade' as she called it which made her body appear very thin. Her movement was hypnotic, and she could easily sense the slightest weakness in your posture or attack. The first thing she told us to do was dance! She said that Silat was based on Indonesian dance, and she taught us how to dance. In fact Johnny and I learned many strange exercises for developing the intention and the power of the mind, as well as for developing the body. In Holland we were exposed to many rare systems of Pentjak Silat.

Ma changed the way I had been doing my forms, teaching me how to open all my postures and to use more spirals. My whole energy changed in Holland, and I began developing my own system, which Ma called Hasilkan Penuh. She taught different things to each student, but much of her teaching was connected to esoteric Christianity. For a long time I had felt drawn to Jesus Christ, but I never knew how to integrate that feeling with my martial arts. Now I began to see my forms as a prayer, as a joyous dance to God. In fact the salutation of Hasilkan Penuh is performed in the shape of the cross and is done with prayer.

We were constantly tested in Holland. Once Ma told us that we were to fight her senior student on the beach the next day. That student was an exceptionally aggressive Harimau Silat expert who would have thought nothing of seriously hurting us, and that night Johnny and I wondered how on earth we would avoid the encounter. The next day came and we all travelled to the beach. Ma drew a large circle in the sand and said that it was to be the fighting arena and that there were no rules to the contest! Johnny went in first against the Harimau expert and within a minute he was badly beaten and had to leave the circle. I went in the circle and I knew that the only way to survive was to open up and have faith. I stood with my arms opened wide, and connected to the senior student. He rushed in but I evaded and countered, all the time keeping very relaxed. I felt the same joy as I had in the underground tournament some time before. Each time he attacked I evaded and countered. When at last Ma called a halt to the fight I had won. I thanked God for showing me the way through and the value of opening to Him and to the attacker.

After some time we left Ma's school. We had learned many good things but in my heart I now knew who my real teacher was - Jesus Christ. When I came back to England I continued developing and teaching the Hasilkan Penuh system. I gave my life to Christ and then my inner life changed for the better. Through my connection with a church I was offered the chance to travel to China to preach the gospel. Along with a small group of Christians I rode on horseback into the mountains of West

China, and I was really impressed with the simple lives of the farming folks. In China I met many martial arts experts. One group of three men really stand out in my mind. Each morning they rose at four o'clock and trained outside this Taoist temple. Their stances were very low and their footwork was so smooth it seemed as if they were gliding. All their movements were in spirals, and even though they moved very slowly it was clear that if they applied their techniques their power was such that it would rip you in two. Their intent and mood was different to anything I have seen before, and to this day I wonder who they were and what system they were doing. They would practice the same movement for a couple of hours, moving in total harmony with each other.

When I returned from China I taught martial arts as a way of pointing to God. Now I feel that martial arts are a good exercise but not a spiritual practice. Only a heart surrendered to God can immerse one in the Living Spirit. Still, Hasilkan Penuh can point to God, so each of our forms has with it a prayer or a story which conveys some truth to the person practicing it. The forms of the ancient styles of martial arts each had a story or song connected to it which gave it real meaning and depth.

Hasilkan Penuh is taught in three stages. The first is the level of the Tree. Picture a seed planted beside a flowing river. Slowly the seed grows into a tall tree, it's roots spreading out in a circle around the trunk, solid at the base but totally flexible at it's tips. After a time it will produce luscious green leaves and fruits. In our practice we develop our stances and footwork, which are our roots, and whilst our stance becomes unshakable our arms and hands stay soft and relaxed like the tips of a tree's branches. Most crucial is the perfect alignment of the feet, knees and body. This level may take a long time to cultivate, but if you have patience you will bear much fruit.

Technically, at this level the student begins with the practice of a series of internal/external exercises which I developed. These are all performed very slowly whilst on the ground, and they especially strengthen the legs, buttocks, and lower back area. Breathing is natural, never forced, and the joints of the body are gently opened and closed whilst a spiralic energy is cultivated through the movements themselves. Then the student practices three stance jurus (short forms) and three ground jurus. Footwork is drilled in the eight directions, both solo and with a partner. You need to develop a strong link with the earth, so that if someone attacks you they feel that they are attacking the earth itself! Emphasis is given to the practice of sampok, or the spiral seated stance, and the practitioner must be able to move out of sampok very quickly into any direction.

Ground fighting is a speciality of this art, and there are over eighty circular kicks, many of which are launched from the ground. To defend against kicks we move in and redirect the leg rather than trying to block it. At the tree level many two man drills are practiced which develop sensitivity and reflexes in the whole body rather than just in the arms and hands. True sensitivity comes from the earth and the stances, not from the upper body.

The second level of training in Hasilkan Penuh is the Deer. Just as a deer thirsts for water, so too my soul thirsts for God. Practice this level with the same intensity as if you were crying for water, with a spirit of yearning to uncover the lessons contained within. In the Tree level one practiced inside a circle, but in the Deer one breaks out of the circle and develops evasive footwork and great springing power. You learn stepping patterns which show you how to evade a multiple attack and instantly face any of the eight directions. With the root and balance gained from the Tree you now cover a large area. The principle of Hajah, or yielding, is integrated into all movements, so that a slight evasion in one direction can prepare you to spring back with great force. In this system power is developed naturally, and comes from the opening and closing motions, the coiling and uncoiling of the whole body. Many Ba Gua teachers have commented on the similarity of our circular evasion steps to the steps of their art.

In actual fighting we allow the attacker's energy to move us. This requires that we open up to the attack and trust in the flow. It requires faith, and that faith only comes from being tested time after time until you have surrendered totally to God's Will. Then he will move you as he wishes. Can you imagine moving in God's hands?

The highest level of Hasilkan Penuh is the Formless Form. The wind blows where it will, no one knows where it is coming or going, and so too we must be totally spontaneous and formless in our movement. At this stage your practice is totally your own and no one else can guide you. You will move naturally, never resisting but always yielding, body/mind/spirit in harmony, with every step a reflection of one's inner nature. Now you have produced the complete martial art within yourself.

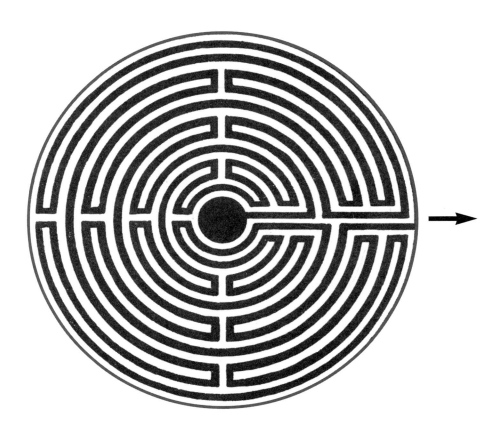

Chapter Three

The Taoist Arts Of Bruce Kumar Frantzis

One of the few Western lineage holders of the Chinese internal martial arts, Bruce Kumar Frantzis has developed a reputation in the West over the past decade as both a proficient fighter and an intelligent communicator of previously obscure internal principles. Born in New York City in 1949, Kumar spent many years Taiwan, Japan and China studying with renowned masters such as Wang Shu Chin and Hung I-Hsiang. It was from his main teacher Liu Hung Chieh, an enlightened master of Taoism and Esoteric Buddhism, that he received a genuine lineage in Ba Gua Chang, Hsing I Chuan and Wu style Tai Chuan. After Liu's death in 1986, Kumar returned to the United States where he continued to teach and write about chi gung, internal martial arts and Taoist meditation.

My first impression on meeting Kumar was that of his strong warrior energy. Sitting or walking, he really fills the space around him with a presence that goes beyond his physical body. Watching him perform his Ba Gua Chang the immediate feeling is one of amazement that such a big person can move so fast and smoothly, or that someone who broke his back in a car accident can spring backwards and forwards with such agility. His book on chi-gung is titled " Opening the Energy Gates of Your Body", and he has recently finished "The Power of Internal Martial Arts" (both published by North Atlantic Books) which is really one of the best books ever written on the subject.

The following interview gives a new and interesting perspective on many aspects of the Taoist internal arts.

(All material in this section is from a tape recording by B. K. Frantzis. Copyright B. K. Frantzis 1997. Photos copyright B. K. Frantzis.)

On Hsing-I Chuan

Hsing-I is about developing a hard, steel-like energy and an extremely aggressive mind. The naturally yang energy of a male can acquire these qualities relatively easily, although they require substantial focusing.

*Bruce Kumar Frantzis receiving instruction
in Bagua from his teacher, Master Liu Hung Chieh.*

The first five techniques of Hsing-I are variants on a single idea, which is to neutralise the power in your opponent's hands and strike your opponent. The first technique, Pi, emphasises downwards energy, while Tsuan is an upwards, rising energy that flows around everything like water. Beng is very straight, representing the wood element as it literally grows out of your body. Pao is like fire, suddenly exploding out to flicker through any holes in your opponent's defences. Heng is the fifth technique, and skilled practitioners will usually admit that it took them ten years of hard practice to begin to understand it. Heng combines Pi, Tsuan, Beng and Pao into one integrated whole, so one must understand the first four techniques very well before even beginning to play with Heng.

Cookbook instructions, such as "your hand goes out, you block and punch", are vastly inadequate for learning to properly execute these five techniques. The fact of the matter is that the cookbook approach alone lacks sufficient substance to work in a real confrontation. To surpass the simplest level of Hsing-I's five primary force vectors and progress beyond the limits of the cookbook approach, a practitioner must radically expand his/her consciousness and access the five elemental energies. This requires you to develop the capacity to project your mind toward your opponent in numerous ways to effectively utilise the energies of the five elements.

In classical Hsing-I, the chi development underlying these five elemental energies involves three successive stages - Ming-Jing, An-Jing and Hua-Jing. Ming-Jing is obvious power, it's strength is readily visible. At this level the practitioner has an understanding of how things function mechanically and how certain movements work, but still has no understanding of the energies of the five elements. With the development of An-Jing, one's power becomes virtually invisible in that your opponent cannot see what you are doing but he can readily feel the power that you generate. At the third stage, your strength becomes completely invisible in that it can no longer be seen or felt - only at this stage, Hua-Jing, do you start directly perceiving the five-element energies. Only then are people actually working with the five-elements that create the world and everything that surrounds us. Few practitioners ever reach this stage.

Of the internal arts, Hsing-I is the most suitable for fighting, because fighting is it's primary agenda. In many respects it is like a super-sophisticated karate, a steel fist in a velvet glove. I still do Hsing-I as a yoga to warm up my body, but I personally do not like the aggressive attitude that it naturally evokes. Few people in the West have practised Hsing-I under optimum training conditions, and thus few have developed it to a level where they could even know if it is easier or harder, or better or worse, than any other martial art. Very few practitioners who studied Hsing-I in the West have ever completed the entire training necessary to be able to do such comparative analyses.

On Tai Chi Chuan

The challenge in Tai Chi is to give up aggression without going into passivity, thus remaining very active, alive and receptive. For males this is an especially difficult task because this quality goes directly against the hormonal rush of violence, anger and aggression. The soft energy of Tai Chi, presuming it is of equal volume, can ultimately prevail over the easier-to-develop hard, steel-like energy of Hsing-I.

Within the Taoist tradition there is a very clear way in which Tai Chi is practised as a path of spiritual development. This path always includes a great deal of meditation as well as martial training. In pursuing this spiritual path, one strives to interweave and unify the martial and the meditational into an inseparable whole.

On Ba Gua Chang

Ba Gua integrates the hard energy of Hsing-I and the soft energy of Tai Chi with a seamless continuity. In Ba Gua you learn to let go of your mind completely and trust that effective martial applications will emerge spontaneously when needed. This capability - to really let go, be spontaneous and seamlessly combine hard and soft - is not easy to develop.

It is not too difficult to become spontaneous if you are only using hard energy. In Hsing-I, for example, tremendous spontaneity and sensitivity can be developed while refining and focusing your aggression. In Tai Chi, it is more difficult to develop spontaneity because you must do so while learning also to bypass your natural fighting aggression without succumbing to passivity. Spontaneity is more difficult in Tai Chi, simply because you are being asked to do a lot more. Ba Gua is even more

challenging than Tai Chi because it includes softness without excluding hardness. To achieve a level of spontaneity that permits flawless, unbroken change from hard to soft and soft to hard requires the complete absence of any hardness or rigidity in your mind.

Another essential quality of Ba Gua is the development of a sense, in your feet and throughout your whole body, of having continuous access to and awareness of all angles on a 360 degree circle around you. Tai Chi and Hsing-I, for comparison, operate only 90 degrees out to either side. The only way you can really access the 360 degrees of Ba Gua is to let go completely in a whole mind-body sense; in doing so, you also abandon any sense of the static, fixed centre found in Hsing-I and Tai Chi. Ba Gua moves completely beyond the static level of awareness into the realm of the continuously dynamic.

Fighting proficiency is a by-product of Ba Gua training, not a primary goal. If you fixate only on developing your fighting proficiency, you will be unable to let go of your mind enough to reach your full potential in fighting applications. Even in a strictly martial type of Ba Gua, the nature of how the practice evolves is such that you will not excel if your sole motivation is to fight well. It is a fascinating and paradoxical situation.

On Meditation

Most people pursue spiritual practices in order to build their sense of identity or simply to feel more grounded in their lives. This pursuit is worlds apart from trying to dive all the way down through the depths of your mind and heart towards a complete awareness of Consciousness itself - what Buddhists call the nature of mind and Taoists call the Tao.

The martial tradition I learned from my teacher Liu, who was a lineage holder in a Taoist sect, comes from one of these more comprehensive spiritual traditions. People use meditation in many martial arts, but they usually treat it as a separate practice, as a helpful supplement rather than an integral part of their training. Taoism is one of the only active religious philosophies I know of which has a highly integrated and truly warrior-transcendent tradition.

Liu first learned meditation within the Ba Gua lineage, for several decades. The founder of Ba Gua, Dong Hai Chuan, taught the Taoist meditation work to only a few students. The majority of his students learned how to throw, kick and strike, but they never learned anything about Ba Gua's meditation tradition. Next, after only three years of intensive Buddhist study, Liu was declared fully enlightened in Tien Tai Buddhism. He attributed this achievement, the rapidity of which was virtually unheard of, to the meditation skills he had already developed in his Ba Gua training. Finally he travelled to study for another decade with a number of Taoists in the mountains of Sichuan Province. Liu also stated, however, that while his Ba Gua training took him close to the end of meditation, Ba Gua alone could not take a person all the way. Taoism itself could - Liu was quite clear about that.

There is a great variety of practices in Taoist meditation that are entirely unnecessary for Ba Gua as a martial art. The fact of the matter is that most people will not do the extra meditation work because their interest lie in martial training alone.

On Violence And Compassion

The fact that the Taoists are not philosophically opposed to war is shown clearly in Taoists texts such as the Art of War. But even though Taoism rejects the principle of non-violence, the Taoist outlook strongly disapproves of unnecessary aggression, such as violence that is gratuitous and wars that are needless or wasteful.

There are some young men who can be characterised as having an abundance of raging hormones that could predispose them to violent behaviour for it's own sake. These urges come from the glands themselves, which are strong, healthy and active at this stage of life. For young people training in the internal martial arts, this glandular-based preoccupation with violence can grow into an artistic obsession. The average person cannot view the manner in which he may injure or kill six people as the equivalent of a great painting - a martial artist can. In the Samurai warrior tradition, the skill of warfare, when it reached it's creative pinnacle, was viewed as a high art. This is very different to the current perspective in the West.

Those who pursue martial arts as a spiritual practice eventually lose the desire to cause harm as this desire becomes unessential to their artistry. Personal obsessions carried over from youth eventually stop motivating

Bruce Kumar Frahtzis showing Single Whip of Tai Chi Chuan.

their work as the spiritual aspects of the practice become more refined. The desire to contact Consciousness itself becomes the new source of motivation, and the need to cause actual harm - gratuitous violence, needless war - is left behind.

Does this transition happen for people who get involved with the martial arts from the fighting side alone, and not as a spiritual practice? It does with a few, but this transcendence is rare even among truly talented martial artists. Many people who have been lauded as the greatest spiritual martial artists were only mediocre in terms of their martial skills. Liu was one of the few exceptions, as was Ueshiba (the founder of Aikido), who approached the highest levels of martial skill before rejecting the need for violence. Besides these two I have met only four or five others. The remaining 99 percent of all martial artists will, when serious pressure is brought to bear, still depend on hormonal aggression to some degree in their martial art practice even when they get older.

The combined practice of meditation and martial arts is what helped me get past an aggressive fixation myself. When I was younger, in my teens and twenties, I loved to fight. Something happened once where I hurt someone severely, and that shook me right to my core. It made me very unhappy, but aggression stayed with me because it had already become a habit. Around the time I was thirty, I underwent experiences in meditation that enabled me to feel my opponent's pain when I hit them. Before that, I would feel my own pain and I would understand that other people were feeling pain, but I had never actually physically felt their sensations of pain and empathised with them. Since I was not of a cruel or capricious nature, this experience increased my desire to back off even more. But the reflexive urge to fight did not stop until meditation cut this obsession off at the very roots in my mind. The habit of needing to engage in fighting diminishes every year. To me, fighting is only a play of energy at this point.

Many exercises in Taoism involve fighting until your emotions go berserk, then stopping to sit and meditate in order to find out where the roots of these emotions lie. Through these exercises you grow away from the reflexive indulgence in those emotions by learning to understand and move past them. Most people who seriously practice martial arts build up an incredibly high level of aggression in order to overcome the fear of engaging an opponent. The problem is that once this aggressive habit is in place, it is with you to stay unless you work purposefully to remove it. Meditation is one practice that can take you beyond this dependence on hormonal aggression. Once you have done so, you reach a whole new level of strength.

On Liu Hung Chieh

Liu had everything, but most remarkable of all was his mind-boggling level of simplicity. I was already pretty strong the first day I met him in Beijing. He was sitting in a chair, I remember, and looked as though he weighed a hundred and ten pounds at best. I put every ounce of my strength against him, but could not move even his finger! But whenever he moved his own finger, it would move me. No games, no tricks - no matter what I did, he did not care. Liu told me then, "There is more to energy than being young and strong. There is also your chi, and your mind. "

Liu was stronger than the others I studied with, but he was not faster. As a matter of fact, his speed was not even very impressive. What I learned about Liu was that he no longer needed speed because he had absolutely transcended it. Most people who can move very fast do so by disconnecting and creating large gaps in their movement and awareness. In the internal martial arts, reaching a level at which everything is one piece and connected is like finding the Holy Grail! Liu had attained this level of skill, and it made speed games seem like child's play in comparison.

It is a strange world you inhabit when dealing with the power and strength that comes from such a high level of consciousness. Above and beyond power, Liu had a degree of smoothness that I had never seen in anybody else. He taught me about the nature of mind and his own martial arts were motivated by intelligent compassion. Being his student was a very rare and valuable experience.

On Chi

If external martial arts develop any chi at all, they tend to develop chi which is neither circular nor continuous in nature. External arts tend to focus and concentrate power in a way that creates what they call in China holes and gaps. One does something. . . there is a gap. . . . one does something. . . . there is a gap. Internal martial arts training involves power development that strives to close these gaps in your chi by making them smaller and smaller until they finally disappear and allow your chi to flow in an unbroken, circular, and continuous fashion.

In the first ten years of internal martial arts training, the primary focus is on developing technique and learning about force vectors. Only in the second ten years do most people really start gaining a deeper understanding of the flow of their chi and what it really means to close the gaps. After this stage a lot of the things start to happen, such as true spontaneity of movement in combat. Because the nature of these practices is completely spontaneous, you can apply them however you want. This was how the internal arts became famous in China -they were quite formidable in the unrehearsed arena, where genuine spontaneity counts most. It saddens me to see that internal martial arts today are degenerating away from the development of this hard-earned, self-enriching quality.

On Teaching And Learning

I trained with Morihei Ueshiba during the last two years of his life. He himself was an amazing martial artist, but Ueshiba suffered from a problem frequently encountered with great artists; much of their greatness comes from natural talent that few others have. As a consequence, they have little knowledge of the teaching methods necessary to pass this knowledge on to others who have less natural ability. The real lineages in China include a highly developed teaching system with which to pass on the methods and principles to others. Such lineages communicate about internal structure and function much more clearly than the systems I observed in my years in Japan.

In order to be a lineage holder, the line of succession must be unbroken from the founder. There are three basic types of student: an ordinary student, a disciple and a lineage holder. The ordinary student usually receives a lot less information than the disciple. A disciple learns certain things and learns them very well. Because they are invested with only certain parts of the teaching however, disciples have no responsibility for passing on the entirety of the teaching to the next generation. The lineage holder however, learns the whole system and becomes extremely competent in each and every part of it. Like any human being, of course, lineage holders shine more in certain areas and less in others.

The process of learning internal martial arts can be likened to the making of a Japanese sword. A mediocre Japanese sword has say three thousand layers of steel that have folded, heated, folded, heated, sealed three thousand times! Some of the better Japanese swords have upwards of twenty thousand layers of steel that have been folded and heated. They all come out the same length and thickness, but there is a huge qualitative difference between someth ing that is twenty thousand layers of steel and something that is three layers of steel! The layers in internal martial arts are not obvious, like "Learn to do twelve hooks in three seconds". Without a good teacher to show you, you would never even know what most of the layers are. Good internal martial arts never fake it - everything is for real whilst remaining completely circular. To truly achieve circular martial arts is an artistic challenge of immense proportions. It is an ever-opening and unfolding process that really is as difficult as painting a Picasso. This is not true for external/linear martial arts (such as karate, the harder styles of kung fu, and tae kwon do) in which you retain a certain level of competence and, if you are lucky, you may stay martially competent for the rest of your life. Usually, your skills diminish with age. The nature of the internal martial arts is such that they enable your skills to grow continuously throughout your life. Many people achieve the first two thousand layers, a feat that takes a lot of hard work, but then they get tired and give up. To gain the deepest levels and highest skills the motivation has to come from inside you. The practice is inwardly-directed and self-motivated - it can't be forced on you from the outside.

I spent ten years in China training and researching and getting right to the bottom of the internal arts. Once I did so, I no longer had reason to stay - I walked out with what I had gone looking for from the start.

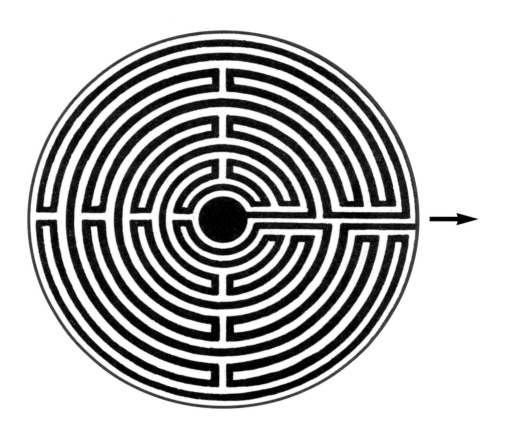

Chapter Four

Grasping The Essence With Eric Lo

When the BBC produced a television documentary on the martial arts some years ago they devoted an entire episode to the teachings of the renowned Taiwanese master Hung I-Hsiang. One young student of Hung's shone like a star as he performed his Ba Gua Chang, turning and swooping down and changing direction with remarkable swiftness and control, and I am certain that it was that performance which led many of us, including myself, to find a Ba Gua teacher. The young man was Lo De Xiu (Eric Lo), and now forty two years old he is an internal martial arts master in his own right with a strong following of both Chinese and Western students in Taipei.

Eric Lo is one of the friendliest and most self-deprecating men I have ever met. During the interview for this book, which he unhesitatingly agreed to despite never having met me before, he explained his ideas and teachings with great energy, humour and insight into the human condition. Watching him teach and perform Ba Gua Chang I was at once impressed not only with his high level of skill, but also with his utter enthusiasm and sense of creativity in teaching. His emphasis is on cutting through the intricacies of the art in order to grasp the essence of the concept or technique at hand. Judging by the ability of his students, he manages to do that very well.

On Learning With The Hung Family

When I was still at school my friend Su Dong Chen took me to the school of his teacher, Hung I-Hsiang, but for the first couple of years I learned mainly basic Shaolin forms and techniques. Still, when I was 16 or 17 I managed to win some fighting tournaments, but even so there was still fear inside me. Hung would tell us very little, just show us exercises and techniques, but from watching the Hsing-I and Ba Gua we could see that it very practical for fighting. Eventually we persuaded Hung to teach us Hsing-I, and then I started to realise the strengths of the internal arts. But still I wanted to absorb the whole of the system passed down by my grandmaster Chang.

Eric Lo demonstrates dragon posture of Hsing-I.

Eric Lo showing application of Bagua style Gao Yi Sheng.

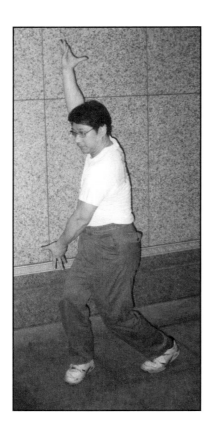

Eric Lo, a student of Hung I-Hsiang who featured in the B.B.C. series 'Way of the Warrior' showing application and solo movements.

I discovered that Hung I-Hsiang and his two brothers had each specialised in a different aspect of the system. From my teacher I got a lot of strength exercises, infighting methods and san-shou. Later I studied with Hung I-Mien who is expert in longer range fighting tactics. Then I met the eldest Hung brother, who was very knowledgeable about the concepts and theories of the internal martial arts. So I really had to research hard, even within that one school, and slowly I pieced together the complete system.

Later, when I was in the navy, I met an old teacher named Liu Chen, and studied a different kind of Ba Gua from him. He really helped me to see the whole range of Ba Gua tactics and techniques, such as throwing, kicking and dien-hseuh (striking vital points). Then I was able to put the training methods and concepts into a well structured system.

If you just blindly follow your teacher you will not reach the highest level of ability. You must think deeply, compare methods and ideas with your fellow students, and do research. Then you will go deeper and deeper into the art.

On Hsing-I Chuan, Tai Chi Chuan And Ba Gua Chang

The five elements of Hsing-I are concepts or keys. Pi-Chuan, for example, is everything coming from up to down. It can be a palm, a hammerfist, or a big takedown technique as in the dragon form. The twelve animal forms take the elements and make them more practical for fighting. I can do the standard Pi-Chuan to aggressively attack you, or use it with a very defensive, scared feeling, as in the monkey form. All that has changed is the mind, the feeling, but the energy is the same.

In Hsing-I we are looking to develop this wave that runs up and down the spine. You can find this easily in Pi-Chuan. Then we want horizontal power. If you do Beng-Chuan enough you will soon find this particular fa-jing.

Many people doing Hsing-I and other martial arts use a lot of emotion to power their movements, but this is not good. We can say that there are three stages of mind : cloudy thinking, feeling, and emotionalism. Cloudy thinking means that your thoughts are scattered, you cannot focus. This is no good. Emotionalism is the other extreme, and in this state you cease to be aware of subtle internal sensations. What we want is the balance, just feeling with awareness. Move slowly, and turn the attention inwards.

Tai Chi Chuan moves like a wave; it specialises in shifting the defender's body back from the attack, using great sensitivity, and then immediately exploding forward with the attack. A Tai Chi expert will be very sensitive to the slightest pressure put on him, the least bit of strength. This skill comes from doing pushing-hands, but not the so-called pushing-hands that we see everywhere nowadays. People are doing it while casually talking with their neighbour! You cannot! Real push-hands we could call 'understanding hands', and it is done with great attention so that you can feel every pressure put on you.

You must examine the Chinese terms that you hear so often to get the real meaning. Gong (hard) and rou (soft) for example, doesn't just refer to you doing hard and soft techniques. It is also talking about you and your opponent. Is he hard, or soft, and in comparison are you hard or soft? Also each posture can contain hard and soft - my Peng (Ward-off) may feel very strong, very hard, to the attacker if he makes contact with it, but if he touches my body I will feel very soft.

Another misunderstood idea is sinking the chi to the dan-tien (the energy centre located just below the navel). This is wrong! It is the I, the mind, which must be brought to the dan-tien. Why? Because when we form a triangle between L5(the fifth vertebra up from the base of the spine), the point under the navel, and the perineum, we make a very stable centre from which to move from. By putting the mind here you can achieve that goal. How can you put chi in your dan-tien? Your chi is all over your body all the time.

Perhaps more dangerous is the idea that if you practice the internal martial arts you will never need to see a doctor. Many masters died at quite a young age because they refused to see a doctor; to save face they claimed that they could cure themselves with their chi. Then complications arose from small problems which could have been remedied, and inevitably the master died. Some of them were just too fat, and their weight gave them problems which affected their meridians and led to bigger problems.

Now I teach only Ba Gua, since it contains within it Hsing-I and Tai Chi. Only Ba Gua covers all the directions, 360 degrees around. Hsing-I and Tai Chi deal with just one direction at a time. Ba Gua contains the most sophisticated martial art principles. Some masters give too many intricate instructions in the beginning. I would rather ask the student to move naturally, whilst adhering to the important internal concepts. It is like the idea of relaxing. If you follow the classical principles of sinking the elbows, dropping the shoulders, rounding the chest, and keeping the head upright, you will be sufficiently relaxed to do the movements. You don't need to become floppy to relax!

Real internal arts follow a simple, step-by-step methodology. It is not right to complicate the process.

On Meditation

Meditation gives the martial artist a peaceful heart, so that he remains calm in the midst of stressful situations such as fighting. It also gives him the ability to instantly focus on one point.

A big problem with the practice of meditation is that it can lead you to withdraw from society. We can easily feel, "Oh, society is so terrible, there is so much chaos, I don't want to be there!" But this is just another extreme. Society is going to carry on with or without you.

When I was younger, I practised Taoist meditation for eight hours a day for nine months. I became so withdrawn that I didn't want to see people or do business. I didn't have the balance. The word Tao can have several meanings, such as the cycle of natural changes in the Universe, or one's own path in life. To me Tao means balance. We should be able to tolerate all situations, even living in society and having relationships, with a peaceful heart.

There is a funny story which illustrates this point. A certain nun went to see a chiropractor for help with her stiff back. The doctor had been recommended by a junior nun who had gained great benefit and healing from his skills. But as soon as the doctor touched this senior nun she began shouting, "Stop! Stop! You can't touch me, you are a man!" Later another nun asked her, "What is the problem? You meditate all day long to have a peaceful heart in all circumstances, and yet you get disturbed when a doctor touches you!"

So we can see that it is very easy for us to repress emotions. At some point they will come out in a big way, no matter if you are a nun or not. Some people repress anger, some sexual urges, and so on. The key point is to cultivate a happy, open attitude to life, and not one of denial.

Meditation is a tool. It can help you to open the energy centres of the brain, such as the pineal gland and the pituitary gland. Then naturally you will experience strange things, mystical powers, but these are just by-products and must not be focused on. It is easy to become unbalanced doing meditation wrongly. You must proceed step by step, from the lower centres upwards.

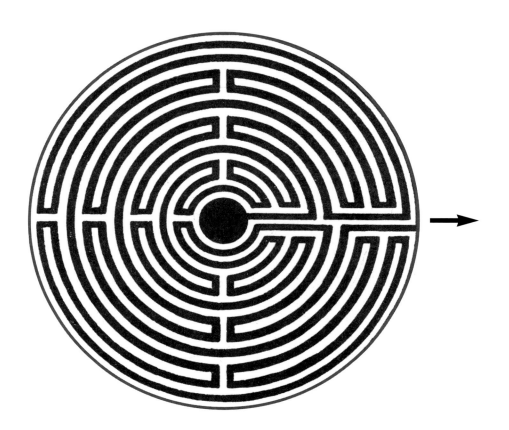

Chapter Five

Masters Of The Phoenix-Eye Fist

Whole systems of Chinese boxing have evolved around specialised hand formations, one of the most renowned of these being the art of Southern Preying Mantis which has as it's central theme the use of the phoenix-eye fist. Considered by many to be a high-level boxing method, Southern Mantis has until recently been jealously guarded by it's practitioners, handed down from master to student behind closed doors. Part of the reason for this could be the devastating implications of a strike with such a hand formation. The phoenix-eye fist uses the extended second-knuckle of the index-finger like a pointed chisel, and it's targets are solely the points of the body which when hit will cause the most damage. Nerve points, blood vessels, energy cavities - the ability to accurately hit such spots with great power was and is the speciality of the Southern Mantis boxers.

Such in depth knowledge of the human body also gave rise to highly effective healing skills, and even in the present day the masters of Southern Mantis are respected as much for their impressive healing abilities as for their fearsome fighting prowess. I was fortunate enough to spend time with two contemporary grandmasters of different branches of this quintessentially southern Chinese art - Ip Shui , eighty-five year old head of the Chow Gar Southern Mantis system in Hong Kong, and Cheong Cheng Leong fifty year old head of Chuka Shaolin in Penang, Malaysia.

The Legacy Of Chow Gar Southern Mantis Boxing

The history of the art begins with Chow Ah Naam who, as a young boy, developed a serious stomach illness and sought help from the monks of the nearby Fukien Shaolin Monastery. One particular monk named Sim Yan treated the boy and over the next few months Chow recovered his health, and subsequently began living full time at the monastery where he began the daily practice of Shaolin Chuan. Being small in stature he sought ways to increase his fighting ability which didn't rely solely on mass and brute strength, and after watching a praying mantis defeat a

(l. to r.) Paul Whitrod, son of Ip Shui, Master Ip Shui, wife of Ip Shui.

bird more than twice it's size he began developing a new way of moving. Along with the help of the aforementioned Monk Sim Yan , the now adult Chow produced an art which harnessed the hidden powers of the body and which used short, quick techniques.

Later Chow Ah Naan taught another monk named Wong Fook Go, and around the end of the Ching dynasty Wong passed on what was now called Chow Gar (Chow Family) Preying Mantis to a young man named Lau Soei. Famed for his superb boxing abilities, Lau Soei was involved in many confrontations which tested his skill. Once, travelling through a forest, he was attacked by a wolf and killed the creature with a single kick to the throat. Another time he was set upon by a skilled martial artist who was unfortunate enough to receive Lau Soei's phoenix-eye fist on a vital point. The man refused Lau's offer of medical assistance and died three months later.

Lau Soei moved to Hong Kong and opened a school, and his successor was Grandmaster Ip Shui who still resides there and who, at the grand age of eighty-five, still revels in letting all-comers test out the steel-like strength of his throat, torso and testicles (which he can suck into his

Paul Whitrod demonstrates a technique of Chow Gar.

body at will) with punches and kicks! He appears skinny and placid, but whenever he move through the techniques of Southern Mantis his eyes blaze with fighting spirit and his fists hit with the heaviness of hammers. He has several uncanny powers which indicate that he possesses a high level of control over his energy, such as being able to extinguish a lighted cigarette on his tongue and also being able to shut off vital points at will so that they are impervious to attack. He is renowned in Hong Kong not only as a boxer, but also for his skill in bonesetting, herbal medicine and the esoteric Buddhist healing system of Wa Fu. Using mantras, mudras and invocations learned from his grandfather (who lived in one of the Shaolin Temples), the Grandmaster has successfully helped to heal people of all manner of serious illnesses, including nervous system disorders and cancer. The healing begins with Ip Shui calling upon the deceased masters of the Shaolin Monastery to come and help the patient, and it seems clear that some kind of energy is being channelled since the patients can be seen responding with jerking movements of their limbs as if they are being shocked by electricity.

Chow Gar Mantis seems to be flourishing in the United Kingdom thanks to the Grandmaster's son and student Ip Chee Keung who taught in London for several years. One of Ip Chee Kung's students back in the mid nineteen-seventies was a fifteen year old boy named Paul Whitrod, who left school obsessed with the practice of the Chinese martial arts. His teacher eventually returned to Hong Kong and was more than a little suprised when Paul turned up on his doorstep one day saying that he had travelled there to continue learn Mantis! The learning wasn't to come easy. The young Englishman's resolve was constantly tested, as he was given the most menial chores to perform every day. For the first six months he practised basic stances, footwork, and the simple eight hand techniques which form the foundation of the art. At night he slept on a hard piece of wood, happily exhausted after a day's practice and oblivious to the airplanes which thundered quite literally overhead as they ascended into Kai Tak airport. It was to be the first of many extended periods of living in Hong Kong for Paul, during which time he became fluent in Chinese, skilled in Chinese medicine and Wafu healing, and learned the whole of the Chow Gar Mantis system under both his teacher Ip Chee Kung and the Grandmaster Ip Shui.

More than twenty years of unrelenting daily practice have given Paul Whitrod a skill and power which has earned him the respect of even the Chinese-born martial arts masters in the U. K. When I first walked into his school several years ago, a single ray of sunshine illuminated a picture of Krishna which hung above the traditional wushu altar and the photos of the Chow Gar ancestors. Ah, a good omen! I thought, remembering Krishna's injunction to Arjuna in the midst of the battlefield of Kurukshetra (where, when all was done, millions of warriors lay dead) to ignore his fears and illusions and to do battle. The Bhagavad-Gita, from where the conversation between Krishna and Arjuna is taken, charts the inner development of man and his relationship with the Divine, and that image on the wall of a wushu school in the East End of London stirred my curiosity. There was a good reason, of course. Paul is a devotee of Krishna in a line of masters which has existed for thousands of years, and he now spends as many hours a day invoking mantras which link him with the Vedic Supreme Personality of Godhead as he does perfecting his boxing skills. His ability and energy with the latter inspire the many students from around the country who train with him, and he seems to be a dynamo of energy as does a two-man drill with a man often much larger than he is, waiting until the student is exhausted before moving on to the next, and then leading them through solo forms and fighting-forms with a speed and power that is thrilling to watch. Whilst many martial artists talk about the location of vital points, Paul has the uncanny ability to hit them with power and grab them with a steel-like grip in the midst of full-speed sparring. He can deliver a strike an inch from it's target with enough force to knock out, and watching him move one can see that he reached that high level of martial ability, the blending of hard and soft into one unified force.

In his younger years Paul experienced the reality of real combat, first in Hong Kong and then later when he began to teach the art in London. He admits to being somewhat wild in those days, but the outcome was that he won each of the fights against both Chinese and Western fighters and learned many lessons in the process. During training he constantly pushes his students on to express more speed and power, to develop more fighting spirit, but he also teaches them the intricacies of Chinese bonesetting and herbology and expounds the values of Vedic philosophy whenever people are interested. Now a calm and happy man in his late thirties he has also spent the past several years learning Hsing-I Chuan from the mainland Chinese master Ji Jian-Cheng, professor of Wushu at Hangchow University.

The practice of Chow Gar Mantis boxing obviously develops great energy and power, as evidenced by the contemporary practitioners of the art, but what exactly are the methods used by them to get these qualities? If I had asked such a question of an adept maybe fifty or a hundred years ago, I would have no doubt come away none the wiser. Luckily the system is now much more open, and the step-by-step training methodology reveals clearly how real 'gung fu' can be developed. As the masters of old kept reminding their students, form without power leads to an old age without skill. Effectiveness in combat is the purpose of Chow Gar, and each exercise manifests a different strength or attribute.

Chai Sau (Grinding Arm)

This is the "battery" of the system, performed by two people and used to develop strong stances, shoulders, forearms and wrists. There are eighteen variations, both static and moving.

Chai Keok (Grinding Leg)

There are nine variations of this two-man drill, which develop hips, knees, ankles and leg strength.

Hay Gung

These are breathing exercises which increase the energy flow inside the body. Chow Gar seeks to unify both internal and external strengths.

How Gung (neck strength)

These are very unusual exercises which toughen and strengthen the neck, jaw and the muscle of the temple on the head. leading to the ability to take strikes to the throat.

Dip Gwat Gung (rib strength development)

These drills unify certain breathing methods with the opening and closing of the joints and skeletal structure of the body, strengthening the ribs and increasing geng power.

Tun Hung (back and spine power)

Through training these drills the adept can emit shock power through his back, useful if one is grabbed or attacked from behind.

Sun Sook Kit (groin training)

This unusual training leads to the ability to suck the testicles up into the body.

Chongs (sensitivity drills)

These vital partner drills develop speed, timing, reflexes, sensitivity and stamina, and may include hitting, blocking, trapping, grabbing and stepping. A central principle in doing these chongs is to keep as relaxed as possible, which aids in responding by feeling rather than purely by sight.

Forms

The forms, or pre-arranged sequences, of Chow Gar, are typically short in length and comprised of rapid combinations of hand techniques done in conjunction with short, rapid steps. The ten basic forms each have three levels of development. Level one is Cho Gen, where the practitioner's strength is said to be "rough". Next is Num Geng, where the power is smoother and more hidden. Finally comes Gen Gen, which is where shock power is manifested with short, sharp contractions and releases. The first form of Chow Gar is Sam Biu Tsin (Three Step Arrow Punch), which involves movements done with both dynamic tension and with speed. This form trains many of the qualities needed by a fighter, including the "iron body" strength. A middle level form known as Sup Baat Yau Long (Eighteen Swimming Dragons) is interesting in that it develops coiling, weaving body motions which avoid the power of the attacker before countering. One moves like a dragon or a fish, flowing freely between the eighteen basic forms in any combination. An even higher level form is Bo Sim Sau (searching for the insect) which uses rapid hand combinations directed to vital points using very aggressive energy.

Fighting Strategy

If the student constantly trains in the above methods with spirit and intelligence, he will have a strong, supple body, good technique and the ability to deliver shocking power over a short distance. Then sparring is undertaken to allow fighting techniques to emerge spontaneously, as well as to cultivate courage and heighten one's sense of timing. Little blocking is done in Chow Gar, rather every motion is aimed at the vital points so that even a block becomes an attack. What is clear from the methodology of this art is that power, conditioning, sensitivity and spirit are just as vital as form and technique.

The Legacy Of Chuka Shaolin Phoenix~Eye Fist Style

Follow the winding stone staircase which leads down from the beautiful Kek Lok Si Buddhist Monastery in Penang, past the pond which is home to dozens of turtles, in between the two rows of shops which sell everything from painted fans to jade jewellery - and you will come to a stone courtyard which for decades has been the head school of the Chuka Shaolin system. Here, on certain nights of the week, you will find Grandmaster Cheong Cheng Leong (affectionately known throughout the Ayer Itam district as Brother Leong), leading his students through the forms and fighting drills of an art which embodies all the traditions and strengths of classical southern Chinese boxing. The Grandmaster is renowned and respected in Penang as much for his remarkable healing skills as for his superlative fighting ability. Known in the Western world as the author of the book "Phoenix Eye Fist", Cheong also had a deep friendship with the late martial art scholar Sensei Donn F. Draeger which led to several high-ranking Budoka visiting Penang to receive instruction in the Chuka art and healing for old injuries.

I had first learned Chuka Shaolin from my teacher, Sean Dervan, many years previously, and was excited at the prospect of training with the head authority of the system. As I flew in from Borneo, and looked down at the long bridge joining the jewel-like island of Penang to the Malaysian mainland⎵ I remembered Sean telling me several years before that Cheong had been seriously ill with cancer. Would the Grandmaster be healthy, I wondered, and was he still teaching a martial art system which required a lot of energy to perform? An hour later I was met at the front of an apartment block by a smiling, dark-skinned man. It was the Grandmaster himself, now fifty-five years old but looking very fit, and on the way up to his flat he told me about the illness which doctors had discovered in the early nineties. The cancer was an egg-sized tumour growing in his abdomen, and

Cheong Cheng Leong - many martial artists made the pilgrimage to his door.

that discovery explained why he had been suffering from blackouts for some time before. Subsequently he had several major operations to remove the tumour, although looking at him training just a few years on from what must have been a traumatic experience it is hard to imagine that this man has ever been anything but healthy. Cheong credits his Chuka Shaolin training with giving him the energy and strength to survive the ordeal and more, to return so soon to normal life. During my short stay in Penang I was treated with great kindness by the amiable Grandmaster, and watched him on his daily rounds giving healing to a whole stream of people suffering from a range of ailments. His speciality is a unique form of massage, using the fingers in a sharp slapping motion which seems painful to receive but is highly effective. According to Cheong such massage uses internal power to bring chi to the effected area of the body. I saw serious muscle spasms and swollen joints being healed after one or two treatments, and many people whose cases have been given up on by conventional doctors have been cured by the

Grandmaster. I met an elderly Taiji teacher who explained to me that following a road accident some years before he was told by doctors that he would never walk again. Dismissing the prognosis Cheong went to the man's house every day for a month, administering the finger-slapping treatment along with herbal medicine. Soon after that the Taiji man was walking normally again. Such incidents seem to happen regularly to Cheong and to his Chuka brother, Tan Hun Poay, who is also famed for his healing skills. Tan regularly travels to Indonesia and distant parts of Malaysia to give healing, and has devoted his life to helping others through the skills which are said to have been developed in the Fukien Shaolin monastery.

The history of Chuka Shaolin begins with one of the survivors of the burning of the Fukien Shaolin monastery, the Buddhist nun Leow Fah Chih Koo, who in the late eighteenth century passed her skills on to two sisters, Chu Meow Eng and Chu Meow Luan. After further developing the art the sisters taught a single disciple, an orphan named Ooh Ping Kwan who followed them with great dedication. Ooh later settled in Canton and taught herbology and martial skills to a small group of students, naming the art Chuka (Chu family) in honour of his teachers. One of the closest of these students was Lee Siong Pheow (1886-1960) who served a long and arduous apprenticeship which eventually led to him developing exceptional skills. Cheong Cheng Leong, Lee's top student and successor, remembers him for the outstanding speed and power of his hand techniques. It was said that no local fighter could defeat him, and he was known for his strictness, high moral standards and his habit of never turning down a challenge to test the Chuka system in combat

After forty five years of daily training in Chuka Shaolin, Cheong moves through his forms with a preciseness and power which mark him out as a master of his art. He stresses the constant repetition of the fundamental drills for those who wish to reach a high level, and his close students exhibit great speed, agility and fa-jing in their practice. Technically Chuka Shaolin is a typically southern Chinese art, with stances resembling those of Hung Gar and handwork very similar to Chow Gar Praying Mantis, and yet like all styles it has something uniquely it's own. The forms are highly dynamic : one moment the exponent is upright, delivering a barrage of strikes and kicks, the next moment he suddenly drops into a kneeling stance and attacks the groin with a tiger-claw, only to spring back up with a series of blindingly-quick palm thrusts. A whole range of footwork patterns are practiced, from triangle steps which teach one how to avoid an attack and then enter the side gate, to circular steps which absorb the incoming force and then lead into a counter-strike or takedown. The phoenix-eye fist is the only closed-hand formation used, and it is trained extensively on a time-tested device called the tsu pai, a paper or rubber board serving as a backing for five circular targets which coincide with certain vital areas of the human body. Elbows and forearm strikes are honed on sandbags, and short-range palm strikes are practised on a rubber board attached to the top of a long plank. The various finger strikes and claw-hands which are seen throughout the forms of the art are done with small weights on the fingers.

The most basic of the fifteen solo hand forms is Kai San (Opening the Mountain), a name which indicates the long and arduous journey which the student will face during practice. The second form, Er Shih Sze Tien (Twenty Four Steps), develops short-palm and claw strikes, and bears close resemblance to Chow Gar's first hand form. Just what the historical relationship is between the various southern Chinese arts is not clear, but obviously a lot of cross-teaching of skills went on in the past couple of centuries. One of Grandmaster Cheong's most advanced forms, and which he has yet to teach to any student, is Shih Ta Hsing Hsian (Ten Animals Fighting Movements), and some of it's techniques are used to

Cheong's power with the long pole was fearsome.

develop internal power. The weapons of Chuka Shaolin include two very powerful long staff forms, spear forms, and sets for the farmers hoe, the iron rulers (the same as the Okinawan sai) and the double butterfly knives. As with the barehand forms there are sets where two adepts face each other in pre-arranged sparring sequences.

It would take many years to learn the complete range of forms in Chuka Shaolin, and in an age when young people have a thousand ways to entertain themselves it is rare to find a student who will dedicate him or herself to learning such an art. Cheong himself commented to me that he wonders about the future of his beloved Chuka Shaolin, although watching his top student Ong Tatt Lin performing an explosively powerful hand form I couldn't help thinking that there will always be someone, somewhere, to take the banner of the traditional martial arts systems. I left Penang warmed by the kindness of the Grandmaster, richer in knowledge and happy to have met yet another human being whose practice was benefiting the world around him.

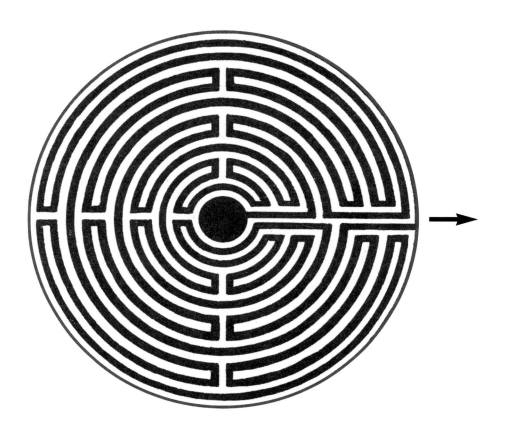

Chapter Six

Bernard Langan – Taoist Arts And Pentjak Silat

I first met Bernard Langan when he travelled to England from California to give a series of Ba Gua Chang seminars, and I was excited at the prospect of meeting someone who had studied both the Indonesian and the Chinese martial arts. Physically much smaller than me, I was impressed at his ability to issue power, his emphasis on correctly aligning the body in every posture, and his internal and external connectedness. I placed my palm on his lower back as he stood in the basic san-ti (three harmonies) posture of Hsing-I Chuan, and as he moved each of his fingers in turn I could feel a different tendon in the back moving. This is the idea of san-ti, that from tips of fingers to toes, everything is connected, and Bernard's manifestation of that principle made it clearer than ever before.

After four years practice of Uechi Ryu Karate Bernard began studying the Taoist internal arts with Bruce Kumar Frantzis, and over the past ten years he has also practiced with several other renowned masters including Eric Lo, Sam Tam and Willem De Thouars (of the Chinese Indonesian Silat Kun Tao system). Here he describes some of his experiences and ideas about martial arts, after which he sets out a detailed overview of Ba Gua Chang concepts and methodology.

On Martial Arts Practice

Ultimately the martial arts are for freedom. Most people are afraid of themselves, so these arts can give us freedom from fear of ourselves. That is why I am involved. They also give us health, self-defence skills, and can lead to enlightenment.

After doing track for six years I decided to do something which got better as I got older. I was also interested in meditation. Bruce Frantzis was someone I had heard about from my fellow Karate practitioners, and he had quite a reputation as someone who could really fight with the Chinese internal martial arts. I moved from the east coast of America to New Mexico to study with him and found that his main interest was in meditation and that he had a lot of knowledge that I wanted to learn. Much of what he had really came from direct transmissions from his teacher Liu Hung Chieh. The way he teaches martial arts opens your heart and mind as well as developing martial skills. The imprint that his teacher left on him is really strong. Because it is a lineage system, his teaching is very systematic. There is built into it a methodology whereby the student, if he has a certain amount of diligence and long-term sustained enthusiasm, will reach a certain level, and then an even higher level.

The way a lot of martial arts are taught turns the student into something like an animal. With Taoist meditation we are trying to get beyond the level of an animal. The core practice of Bruce's martial arts is basically Taoist meditation, a way to build a fine passage for your subtle energies which takes your body to a place where you can start to do Taoist Alchemy. Martial arts is, in a sense, a game for kids. It gives you a clear sense of power, of how your body works, of self-confidence, but with the meditation you start to do something else.

I usually teach from an awareness point of view. Chi is something that everybody has but they don't realise they have access to it. Usually when I talk about chi I mean the movement of the awareness, the movement in the mind that is causing the corresponding physical effect. When I am doing something really well I am so quiet that I don't feel chi. . . . . if you are feeling something moving then often it is just surface stuff. The more the mind opens, the more the chi can follow. We do certain practices where we take the I, or intention, and drop it into the heart centre. The feeling of compassion becomes more of an experience which grows out of your practice, rather than something which you concentrate from the beginning as with Buddhism. Compassion seems to arise naturally when you do Taoist practice, and so you can take people who never had any interest in developing compassion, and through the martial arts they will change.

I did a full-moon Taoist meditation retreat with Bruce Frantzis where he guided us through all of the eight bodies of the Taoist system. That was the highlight of my martial arts career, and during the retreat some strange things happened. It was a quiet time of night when we reached the third energy body, which corresponds to the trigram for wind, and suddenly the wind came up. When we reached the fifth, or causal body, a bob-cat killed a rabbit at the bottom of the hill, and we had to look at

Bernard Langan demonstrates a throw on the author.

that point at what needed to die that year in order for new things to come. That is when I realised who I was going to marry!

It has also been very interesting for me to study with Willem de Thouars of Kun Tao Silat, in terms of better understanding the things I was already doing. He is a small man but very strong. Once when I met him at the airport he was carrying two big suitcases, swinging them up into the air and then catching them again. I tried to lift one but it was really heavy. At his work place, instead of using a machine, he carries these big steel bars in his arms! The rest of his family, who practice Indonesian Silat, imagine that he does some kind of magical practice because he is so skilled, but the key is that he does the Chinese internal arts as well as Silat. He cured himself of cancer using chi-gung. There was a time when he used to emphasise the hard Kun Tao methods with his students, but now I feel that he would rather just give his life experiences, like a darshan (meeting of minds).

When Willem de Thouars was younger and living in Indonesia he reached a point in his practice where he had beaten many Silat fighters. His teachers said, "We are going to take you to meet someone really good!", and they took him to where a forty pound monkey was chained to a pole. They told him that he had to fight the monkey. Willem relates it like this. . . . "I went to punch the monkey, but he grabbed my arm and scratched me and bit me! I went to kick him and he clawed me. . . . the monkey beat me! He had beaten many people!"

Willem told me that when he had that fight the energy of the monkey went inside him.

Another very skilled Hsing-I man is Kenny Gong of New York. He is a very down to earth and practical fighter. Once, when he was training in China as a young man, his master told him that in the room next door there was a very special man waiting to teach him. Kenny went to the next room and found a monk floating in the air. He returned to his master and said, "What good is that, I want to fight!"

I went to see the guru who was Bruce Frantzis's yoga teacher in India. He was doing a lecture on the Ramayana (an ancient Indian tale relating the deeds of King Ram and his topmost devotee, Hanuman). Bruce had told me that he progressively goes directly into your consciousness whilst doing whatever it is he is doing. . . . chanting or lecturing or whatever. The guru was talking about Hanuman, and he said that Hanuman wasn't really a monkey, just maybe tails were fashionable in those days! He was making jokes and I was laughing, but no one else there laughed! Half way through this lecture I started thinking. . . . . this man has a lot of energy, I wonder what would happen if I attacked him?

Then I wondered why I would be thinking such a thing! I realised that a lot of people are afraid. If I wasn't afraid I wouldn't want to attack the guru. I sat with that idea. I found that a lot of martial arts people have a lot of fear that they don't want to acknowledge.

Ba Gua Chang - The Eight Trigrams Palm Style

Ba Gua Chang is a profound and spiritual martial art and in China it is considered to be the most unique, beautiful and effective of all the martial arts. It is the rarest of the three internal martial arts with the fewest competent instructors worldwide. It was first taught publicly a century ago by Tung Hai Chuan, who would only say that he learned it from a Taoist hermit in the mountains.

This fluid, circular art places the same emphasis on longevity, relaxation, internal energy development, healing and meditation as does Tai Chi Chuan and can be more effective in self-defence especially against multiple opponents. The basic practice method of Ba Gua consists in walking in a circle and executing unpredictable flowing movements derived from the eight energies represented by the eight trigrams of the I-Ching. The trigrams are associated with the energies of heaven, earth, wind, thunder, fire, water, mountain and lake.

Ba Gua makes the body extremely strong and flexible. It uses both hard and soft energy techniques, always in the context of moving continuously, never stopping in any one place for more than a fraction of a second. Although Ba Gua fist work is very sophisticated, 90 percent of it's techniques use the open hand. With it's tremendous fluidity, power, grace and rapid changes, Ba Gua requires the highest level of discipline, physical co-ordination and effort of the three internal arts. It is also an elegant self-defence system for women. Learning Ba Gua gives the experienced martial artist a rare opportunity to understand highly refined spherical techniques and strategies for fighting eight opponents at once.

Ba Gua is based on Taoist meditation and the practical realisation of the subtle workings of the I-Ching in an individuals body, mind and spirit. A skilled practitioner can manifest the eight primary energies of the universe in their body and understand how these energies change in the cosmos and their relationship to the specific palm changes and the framework within the Taoist conception of the body and the universe. The Taoists believe that the human body as part of the universe is also composed of combinations of the eight energies responsible for the spirit and the different bodies that every human being has : the physical body, the energy body, the emotional body, the mental body, the psychic body, the causal body, the body of individuality and the body of the Tao. The Taoists also believe that the whole of the universe is represented inside every human being's body. They maintain that the mind of a human being is capable of manipulating the eight energies that are inside the body so that they resonate with the energies of the universe which are outside the body. By developing the ability to simultaneously delve inside the body and have direct experience of what is outside the body, one begins to understand what the eight energies of the body are and how they change. From this understanding one comes in time to understand that which does not change, which is called Tao.

Ba Gua is a celestial martial art. A high level practitioner uses the energy of the celestial objects, stars, planets, etc. and the movements of Ba Gua correspond to the way that celestial objects constantly rotate and spiral in orbits around their own centre and around the centre of objects and the forces outside of themselves. Tai Chi uses the energy of the earth and Hsing-I uses the energy of the five elements.

Taoist nei-gung sets from the Ba Gua, Tai Chi or Hsing-I lineage teach an authentic methodology for the complete development of internal healing, martial and (meditational) spiritual aspects of these arts. Taoist nei-gung practice is comprised of sixteen basic segments that form the essence of a solid training program that will allow an individuals practice to reach full fruition and realise the higher potentials of the internal martial arts

These basic segments include :
1. Opening and closing all the physical body's tissues (joints, muscles, soft tissues, internal organs, glands, blood vessels, lymphatic pumps, cerobrospinal system and brain) and subtle energy anatomy.
2. Bringing energy up and down the central energy channels of the body.
3. Manipulating energy of the external aura outside the body.
4. Making circles and spirals of energy inside the body.
5. Moving chi to any part of the body at will especially the glands, brain and internal organs.

6. Projecting energy from any part of the body.
7. Absorbing energy into any part of the body.
8. Connecting every part of the physical body into one unified energy.
9. Stretching the body from inside out.
10. Dissolving blockages of the physical, emotional and spiritual energies.
11. Feeling, moving and transmuting internal energies.
12. Moving energy through the secondary and meridian channels of the body.
13. Gaining control of the left and right (collateral) energy channels of the body.
14. Gaining control of the central energy channel of the body.
15. Learning to use the three elixir fields, or dan-tien, of the body.
16. Absorbing energy into the spine.

Ba Gua as a personal practice has been transmitted through five methods
1. Instruction in physical movement technique only.
2. Nei-gung practices integrated into the walking and self-defence techniques.
3. Instruction in physical technique coupled with direct energy transmissions from master to disciple, but not to ordinary students.
4. Physical instruction coupled with psychic transmissions in which the Hsien, or non-corporeal enlightened immortals of the Taoist lineage, channel energy to the practitioner. This energy produces physical and energetic movements in the practitioners body if one is willing to accept the transmissions and does not block them.
5. Physical instruction coupled with training in Taoist internal alchemy and meditation practices including the use of the five elements and environmental forces.

Chapter Seven

Chris Chappell And The Esoteric Tibetan Martial Arts

For many years I had heard that the Himalayas, the highest mountain range in the world, were home to various sophisticated and esoteric systems of martial arts. Certainly India has had a long history of warriors and martial heroism ; it's great classics of sacred literature such as the Ramayana and the Mahabharata relate myriad tales concerning mystical fighters like Hanuman, Arjuna and Bhisma, and they are a mine of lessons about spirituality and devotion to God from the perspective of both the warrior and the less-martially inclined seeker after Truth

I was fortunate enough to witness a display put on in an English Hindu temple by a group of Indian martial artists hailing from the northern region of Bengal. They were members of an ancient lineage of Ksatriya (warrior caste) devotees of Lord Krsna, and clad in black robes and exuding a strong martial energy they stunned the assembled devotees with fighting sequences which pitted sword against staff and empty hands against various weapons, all done with ferocious speed, power and intent. I was left in no doubt that these men were ready to do real battle, and it wasn't too hard to imagine them fighting on the field of Kurukshetra (where the sacred Bhagavad Gita was spoken) five thousand years ago. Like those ancient warriors, these modern-day holders of a now dying-tradition imbue all aspects of their practice with mantras (sacred sound vibrations which harness spiritual powers) and yogic meditations.

Nestled in the high Himalayas, Tibet too has had a long history of martial arts. For over a thousand years the Buddhist religion has played a central role in every aspect of Tibetan society, and sometimes 40 percent of the male population were living as monks and devoting themselves to spiritual practice at any one time. There were various types of monks living in the thousands of monasteries scattered across the land, and one particular type was the Dob-Dob or warrior-monk. As well as protecting the monastic properties and taking care of the animals, the Dob-Dobs would escort officials and members of the aristocracy on the long journeys which would often need to be taken. Training began from the age of fourteen and included both armed and unarmed fighting methods, as well as internal power development and meditation. They were famed for their bravery, fighting skill and sense of justice.

Over the centuries certain of these martial arts systems became methods of spiritual development in their own right, and martially they were tried and tested in many a bloody encounter with the bandits who plagued the pathways of Tibet. The Dob-Dobs absorbed many other martial arts, including the systems practised by the nomadic tribesmen of the highlands (who were often influenced by the shamanic Bon religion which pre-dates Buddhism in Tibet), and various methods from India and China. Thus the martial arts of Tibet became highly sophisticated and combat-effective. Even today, though, these systems are extremely difficult to locate and access, not least because the Tibetan practitioners themselves recognise that these are very powerful skills which could easily be misused. In Taiwan, for example, I spent time with a certain Kenpo (the official title for an Abbot of a monastery) who had trained since his youth in a martial system which was passed down in a direct lineage from the famed Tibetan Buddhist yogi Milarepa.

It took more than an hour of conversation before he would even begin to discuss his system, and then only in the loosest of ways. Eventually I discovered that the Kenpo had only ever taught a couple of his monks the basics of the art, deeming it far too dangerous to give to outsiders. The first level of the art was a series of chi-gung exercises which vigorously worked the physical and energy bodies and prepared the student for more advanced practices with subtle energies. The next level was a sequence of spinning, whirling movements which could be applied as evasions or strikes depending on the need. The Kenpo told me of the sacred dances performed by Tibetan monks, where the dancers will spin and whirl for long periods of times, much in the manner of the famed whirling dervishes of the middle-eastern Sufis. He said that such dancing created a vortex of energy which, if an outsider tried to enter into, would cause him to spin off with dangerous consequences for his physical and energetic health.

On the subject of whirling energy, the most stunning dance performance I ever witnessed was by a group of whirling dervishes from Turkey. Accompanied by hypnotic sacred music, the first member of the group to stand up was a young boy, dressed in a long white robe, who took

Kun-nye Postures

1

2

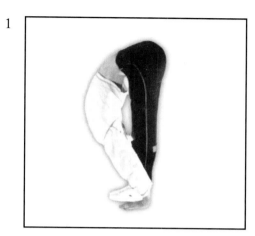

3

centre stage and slowly began to turn anti-clockwise. His feet moved in an incredibly tight circle which kept him on exactly the same spot all the time, as his arms stretched out to either side of him with the palms facing upwards in the manner of Ba Gua Chang's heaven palm exercise. Faster and faster he span until he was really just a blur, the music keeping the ever quickening rhythm. Fifteen minutes later he was still spinning until suddenly DA!! The music stopped and the boy stopped at precisely the same moment, and the boy was facing directly forward towards the audience on the very spot he had began dancing! He stood very still for a short while, returned to his chair and sat quietly, moving only to wipe the sweat from his head. I can only imagine that his energies at that point were spiralling upwards through his body, for he certainly looked ecstatic.

At the present time two Tibetan martial art systems are being openly practised in England. The first is Dord Jee Lam Teb, an art developed by Drukay Rinpoche, an accomplished scholar and monk in ancient Tibet who studied many different martial arts systems from both the Dob-Dobs and from teachers in other countries. Although not a Dob-Dob himself his skill was such that he was sought out by many of the warrior-monks to be their teacher. The forms of the art are related to the lines and shapes of a mandala (a geometric pattern used as an aid in meditation and visualisation), and the concepts and keys come directly from the Kalachakra (The Wheel of Time), an important Tibetan sacred text which describes an understanding of the nature of time, space and the forces of nature.

The second Tibetan martial art being openly practiced in England is Lung Ta, a Bon system which comes from one of Tibet's nomadic tribes. My friend Chris Chappel, who is a teacher of the Chinese internal arts under Bruce Frantzis and Bernard Langan, learned Lung Ta from the man who brought the art to Britain. In the following passages, Chris talks about his experiences with both the Tibetan and Chinese martial arts. He is one of the most friendly and introspective martial artists I have met in England.

Experiences And Teachers

I practiced Wado-Ryu Karate from the age of twelve, and after seven years of that I turned to Kickboxing with Steve Morris, where I was the

senior student and took part in professional bouts. Then in 1983 I began Yang style Tai Chi with Master Chu who is very skilled and strong.

When I met my Tibetan style teacher in 1987 he told me to attack him, and as I did so I felt myself becoming very emotional. I began crying. I didn't expect this at all, because I was a trained fighter and very confident. He had the ability to work on a seemingly non-physical level, to cut through my attack in a way that exposed my core feelings. His art was Lung Ta, and the tribe that was noted for this art in Tibet were famed for the emotional damage which they would do to an opponent. What they would leave in the end was an emotionally wrecked person.

Lung Ta is a Bon system, and the impression I got with my teacher was that he was channeling energy. Unlike many people who channel higher energy he appeared to have access to it at will, which I couldn't understand. I have heard it said that channelled energy is not a hundred percent reliable and can run out, which you do not want in a fighting situation. Although there is much suggestibility which comes from any student who holds his student in awe (I-Chuan and Yang style Tai Chi are examples of systems where over suggestibility of the student is a barrier to progress), my teacher's techniques were not physiologically dependent on wiring up the student's nervous system through physical structuring but rather appeared at times to work directly at the level of perception (mental/psychic). He had amazing abilities with the mind. He could make his energy very diffuse, so that as you attacked him you became disorientated and had no place to focus on. Or he could become extremely one-pointed so that you felt very scared to go near him. He specifically worked with the third-eye centre and the heart centre.

Technically Lung Ta comprises four forms, each of which has eight changes. They are done whilst walking a circle, as in Ba Gua Chang, using various mudras and visualisations. The idea of the first form is to locate the Windhorse, or the primal energy of the universe, and then to let it go. We would do many practices where we would fight in order to bring up the emotions, and then we would take those emotions back into the form. Going in this way from form to fighting and back again teaches you many things about energy.

I got into a lot of psychic work and invocational work, and such work is designed to still your mind. It is not meant as a permanent practice. It gets you out of your conscious mind and makes you aware of energy that you wouldn't normally be aware of. Deities are personifications of energy which exist in the universe but which are personified by certain traditions. The more you practice and become aware of different levels of energy, the more you see that everything is the same. In the beginning we always see the differences, but later you see the similarities

I met Bruce Frantzis in 1987, going to see him after hearing that he was very tough. After doing a workshop with him suddenly a lot of pieces which I had spent three years thinking about fell into place. I realised that there was a way of breaking down chi-gung components, understanding them and then letting them go, but knowing how to consciously recreate them. There was no hit or miss about Bruce's method. It was a direct hit every time.

Bruce's Ba Gua is exceptional, and it is coming in a direct lineage from Dong Hai Chuan. When Dong brought Ba Gua to Beijing no one could beat him or his student Yin Fu. These men had a level of skill which went beyond the physical. It was a period, around the turn of the century, when all of the skilled people hung out together and cross-referenced their skills. I feel this is so important for us to progress, the idea of comparing and sharing training methods. In terms of actual combat, the Ba Gua was often used to kill people. It was very efficient as a fighting method.

Bruce's eight palm changes each work a different energy body:

- 1st palm works the physical body.
- 2nd palm works the energetic body.
- 3rd palm works the emotional body.
- 4th palm works the mental body.
- 5th palm works the causal body (karmic body)
- 6th palm works the psychic body.
- 7th palm works the body of individuation, which is how all the bodies integrate to form you.
- 8th palm works the Tao body, where you no longer need a teacher.

You have to experience these things on a deeper and deeper level and then you could get it from Tai Chi or Yoga, as long as that system doesn't become a trap. The most simple things can have the biggest effects.

Ba Gua is not for the masses. For one it is physically demanding on every level, because each time you do it you are going through the eight bodies, through different transformations, and pulling up energy that often people don't want to deal with.

Sometimes you can get trapped into thinking that you are someone special. I got trapped like that with the Tibetan Lung Ta practice. I began to imagine that I was on to something really unique. It is okay, as long as you are aware of the tricks you are playing on yourself. Then you can let go of them. The idea is to have a path of no path, and that is the Way of the Taoists - you have a way but it is really no way. But this is so cryptic and logically impossible to understand that you are left with only one option and that is to do the practice. Then it becomes a realisation and you cannot explain it in words. But just because no one else describes it as you do does not invalidate the experience.

Another point is to enjoy the practice, because if you take it too seriously you must have an egotistical reason for doing so. If you can just enjoy it you will suddenly find that your own level has gone up and you wonder how you got there. It was just that you were not getting in your own way! It is also important to have a teacher who embodies what they teach. They often will not say a lot, they just show you by doing and maybe one or two words and then you go, "Ah!". It changes your way of thinking. They can transmit it non-verbally.

Bruce Frantzis is a man who has had to use his skills. He has gone through a lot to learn his arts and has overcome many obstacles. He has returned to the West and now he is going to talk about it. If Grandmaster Liu Hung Chieh had passed the arts on to someone who was just going to sit in a cave all his life, it would have been of no benefit to mankind. Liu filled in the pieces of the jigsaw for Bruce and made it a coherent reality. Bruce really has a totality of understanding about each of the systems he teaches and can clearly manifest the varying mindsets and energetic qualities of Hsing-I, Tai Chi and Ba Gua, and can go from one to another. This is an incredible achievement. I have not seen anyone else who can separate the energetics of the three arts without them all looking and feeling the same.

A big question I had when I was doing Lung Ta is how compassion relates to martial arts, because that art is based on opening the heart centre. After studying with Bruce I now understand that the heart/mind practices are the highest level of Ba Gua. Heart/mind practice is about doing what is needed. On a karmic level you could be creating future suffering for yourself by inflicting pain on someone. The Shambhala model is that compassion is a great thing, idiot compassion is not. You can be compassionate to another human being, but when someone is bent on destruction and it is coming for you then you have a choice to survive or not. We are born with an innate survival system in our bodies, we want to live, we don't want to die. That instinct is very pure and is connected to higher consciousness, Tao, or God.

I find it difficult to equate fighting with compassion on one level. . . . but on another level I am a human being. It comes down to the intent. If through necessity you damage another human being that is quite different to neurotically murdering someone. I asked Bruce how he equated his violent past with what he is doing now. He said, "I have done what I have done, and that is it. " I could see that he has no regrets about what he has done, good or bad. Therefore he is free to get on with his life.

Most people walk around at sixty or seventy still dealing with things from their childhood. In shamanic traditions you always had this point of going from a child, and the neurosis of a child, to being a man. We think that being a man means being a hard-case, but it is not, it is really about understanding your own fears and letting them go, and knowing that now your whole perception of the world is going to change because you are going to be a hunter-gatherer and a warrior. It is a different mentality to the people nowadays who imagine they are warriors. They are not warriors, these martial arts people! In my mind the warrior is the guy who has a fruit stall, who does his own spiritual practice and who can use his skills in a fighting context. He survives when he needs to but is compassionate when he needs to be. It is very different to people who try to put on a suit of armour and think, "I am tough!" because that is another crutch. I know because I have done it. I have worn the karate mask, the kickboxer mask, the eclectic martial artist mask that I thought I had. It's all illusion!

When you reach the Tao body, whatever that is, you are beyond good or bad, beyond punishing yourself. One man I know was trained by Idris Shah (the renowned Sufi teacher and writer) and was given permission by him to teach years ago. I told him, "Baba, you are one of the few people I know who is wealthy but happy. Most of the wealthy people I know are miserable. How is that ?"

He said, "I have never planned anything. Everything in my life just happens. I am open to it. I have no regrets about anything that has happened in my life, good or bad. It is my life and I can't regret my existence. So I have done some bad things and some good things, but I can't regret my mistakes."

What I got from that man was a sense of freedom. It is quite a state to go beyond regret.

Lung Ta - Psycho-Physical Dur Bon PRactices

Lung Ta is a Dur Bon Psycho-Physical practice involving processes of awakening consciousness in ourselves by making us aware of the heart centre. The basic practice is circle walking. From this walking practice develops an experiential awareness of the circular and spiral nature of energy.

The term Lung Ta is translated as Windhorse. If you were talking about a person's windhorse you would be referring to the person's life force, their energy and spirit. When you walk the circle you are walking the edge of creation , the line between life and the void. The goal of the practice is to awaken one's windhorse , to awaken the heart that is at war with itself.

Through the psycho-physical forms of this system one is earnestly searching to develop the quality of being present to the energy of the heart centre. To move from the primordial heart and connect with that which links all consciousness. The physical forms are energetic structures which channel Universal energy (the Bon religion regards itself as the Universal religion.) as well as the energy manifested in physical form.

There are similarities in the Lung Ta system to Ba Gua Chang. The Chinese system follows the Taoist method of cultivating a strong physical level of awareness and moving up to the Tao-body level. The Tibetan method in comparison works directly at the level of the heart in the belief that the heart -centre practice is the most balanced point from which to develop oneself. Practising with the heart-centre ensures that you don't become hooked on power and that equally you don't intellectualise the experience of your practice.

Historical And Religious Background

The Lung Ta practice was taught in exile by Urgyen Gnam Chak. Gnam Chak translated means sky-metal and is the name of the clan. Known as the Bon masters they were nomads who historically migrated between Mongolia and Tibet. The Gnam Chak's practices came from the Dmu clan which was part of the Lha-rigs (God-spirit) lineage. The Lha-rigs practiced ritual and ceremonial magic and were renowned for their psychic powers. Even though the Lung Ta claims to be a teaching of the pre-Buddhist tradition, it has aspects of both the old and the new systems of Bon.

Lung Ta practice develops the Dmu chord connection which is sometimes referred to as the sky chord. This sky chord is your connection to the Cosmos and the Universal life force, the connection of man's consciousness to supreme consciousness. Mercia Eliade, in her book 'Shamanism - Archaic techniques of Ecstasy' states , Bon traditions further speak of a clan, Dmu , a name that at the same time designates a class of Gods. These dwell in heaven and the dead go to them there by climbing a ladder or rope. Long ago on earth there was a class of priest who professed to have power to guide the dead to heaven because they were masters of the rope or ladder. These priests were the Dmu.

The Bon Po priests differ in no way from real shamans ; they are even separated into 'white' Bon Po and 'black' Bon Po. According to Buddhists the white Bon are the result of the influence of Buddhism, but then according to Buddhist historians the Bon religion also plagarised Buddhist texts. There is substantiated evidence that in several recorded instances the Buddhist texts have been copied word for word from Bon texts. Therefore I view the claim that white Bon developed due to Buddhist influence with the proverbial pinch of salt. It has an echo which sounds rather like the claims of Christian missionaries that all the tribes they influenced were savages, lacking in the grace of the divine teachings.

Kum-Nye

As well as the basic circle walking practice there are Kum-Nye (postural exercises) which strengthen the energetic and physical bodies and also strengthen the intent of the individual.

Drahla - Higher Energetic Practices

Drahla is energy in all it's forms. Everything has a vibrational frequency, everything is drahla. Drahla exists in visible and invisible forms. The drahla practitioner develops the ability to feel drahla, to connect consciously and become aware of the previously hidden aspects of reality. The Drahla master was also referred to as the 'Dancing master'. He would imbue his forms with the forces of drahla. He would invoke the elements, animals, archetypal forces and deities. It was critical that drahla practice was only taught to people who had the emotional stability to safely balance the energy that is invoked. I have personally been on the end of an attack by someone who had invoked a deity without instruction or guidance. He exhibited psychotic behaviour and was clearly out of control

Developing the Heart and Mind in the Context of Fighting

Fighting in the Lung Ta tradition is symbolic of the inner battle that rages within the human mind/body. By facing aggression one aims to spontaneously focus all the drahla that permeates one's being and for it to co-exist with the energy that enters your personal energy field. This has the effect of you not existing within the normal experience of existing. In other words, if all I am is drahla and that drahla occupies space and time in the same way that everything else does, then I am that which is attacking me. Therefore I don't exist and you don't exist

If you believe and experience a you that is fighting then you are stuck in the gross world, you are subject to the limitations of phenomenal existence. The heart of the system is your own heart, the Universal heart and mind. Developing heart starts with walking the void, just as everyday we sit, eat, talk, sleep, hear, see, smell and touch the void in every waking moment. Our mortality is our gift, and our greatest teacher. To know war is to know peace, and one has to accept the war that rages in our heart, so that we are not enslaved within the physical body. We all walk the void and we are inherently composed of light. We are the dancers of light and we walk the circle of light on the edge of the abyss of creation. We walk through life and balance precariously on the edge of physical death.

The 14 Breaths

These are breathing exercises designed to alter one's consciousness and to awaken further sensitivity to subtle energy, and are practised whilst walking or sitting. Vibrational qualities are established as sensitivity to the breaths develops. This has the effect of changing the feelings in the brain and the organs of the body. As a result the energetics change and these energetics can be used in application of fighting techniques.

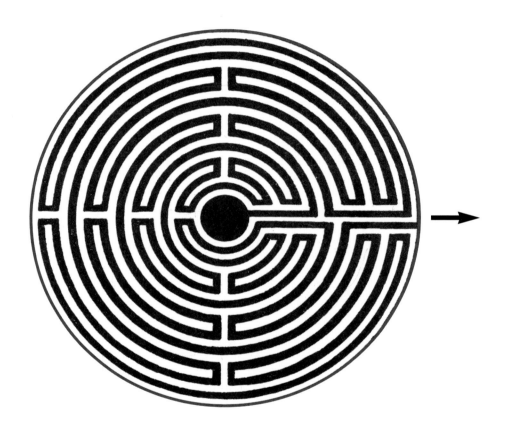

Chapter Eight

The Three Special Teachers Of Chris Demwell

I came upon a new martial arts school in the North of London by chance, and as I walked up the staircase leading to the main are I sensed a definite Buddhistic energy. Behind the reception desk sat a stocky, black haired man of Italian descent who greeted me with a strong Birmingham accent and a warm smile. Chris Demwell was a placid-enough looking man, but as we began talking I discovered that his life had been far from ordinary and that, like myself, he accepted the realm of the mystical as our natural birthright. I instantly liked the man for his unpretentiousness and self-deprecating humour. Over the next couple of months we were to share many deep and winding conversations about the esoteric aspects of the martial arts, and our relationship coincided with yet another shift in energy which ultimately led me to return to study in the Far East.

This is the story of Chris Demwell, who now lives in Hong Kong, and his three special teachers.

I was raised in a Chinatown in Birmingham, England, and from a young age I studied Chinese martial arts such as Hung Gar and Southern Mantis Boxing. At the age of nineteen I went to Hong Kong and studied the Yau Gung Moon system with Master Ho Tak Kin. It was his grandfather who founded the art after studying with a Shaolin monk. I would rise at five o'clock every morning and spend a few hours training and practising the lion dance. After several months of this I noticed that I was feeling very supple, soft and clean internally. Yau Gung Moon is a very beautiful and powerful system which gives you these qualities.

Later I went to Taiwan and then back to Hong Kong for a year, and in those places I was doing a lot of hard style chi-gung and fighting. I noticed a lot of heat building up in my body from this, and in fact such practices can be dangerous to the health if not done regularly and correctly. It was in Hong Kong that I had the most painful experience of my life. Something had come inside of me, what the Chinese call an 'Above Master'. I thought at the time that I was going mad. In desperation I went to a Catholic church, but they wouldn't help me.

Eventually a Buddhist lady in our village came and exorcised me. I was very fearful of her, and it really felt like being burned alive. I felt as if something came out of my chest, and then afterwards I was fine. You could say that I had been possessed by the spirit of a departed master. Such things are not uncommon in China, and the people accept the reality of these matters.

Later on I spent a year in Beijing, and there my character changed for the worst. I should explain that there are four classic books which, according to the Chinese, should be read in a very specific order. Young people should read the Three Kingdoms since it will motivate you to do something good for society. Then you read the Journey to the West (the story of the Monkey King) which discusses religious ideas. In your forties you read Water Margin, because it is about martial heroes and is very violent, and by then you are not effected by that kind of thing. Later in life you read Dream of the Red Chamber, which deals with sex. Unfortunately, I read Water Margin first! I got in a lot of trouble fighting. I started eating a lot of meat and drinking a lot of wine, just like the characters from the book. It made me very depressed, since my higher-self knew that I was doing wrong. This kind of thing is a downwards spiral.

Whilst in China I met a certain Korean man who had trained in an old Korean martial art system. He had been in the special forces, and after leaving the army he turned to Buddhism and walked up and down Korea for five years without touching money. He was very strong with fiery eyes, but I was very impressed because he could be so gentle. Before breakfast he would punch and kick the wall a thousand times, and each time the building shook. He hated injustice. When ever we went out to drink he would really explode if he was pushed too far, but he only ever beat people who deserved it.

I had damaged my wrist whilst fighting, and after a month it was still not healed so I went to an army hospital in Beijing to find a doctor. Once there I saw this interesting looking guy staring at me, and though I had never seen him before I knew at once that he was the chi-gung doctor I had been told about. We became friends, and I would often watch him doing acupuncture for people. He taught me a chi-gung exercise which, after much practice, gave me a feeling of water-like energy inside. One night in my room, while I was reading, I noticed spirits walking around the room. I got very scared, and stayed in a friend's room for three nights without moving out.

Chris Chappell showing Lung-Ta.

I went back to the doctor and explained what was happening, but he said it was normal. He took me to see his own teacher, a peasant who lived in a village in the middle of nowhere. The old man had no possessions, grew a few vegetables, and the only decoration in his simple house were a few pictures of the Buddha which he had painted himself. He sat me down and patted me   I returned to my University at 5 p. m. I slept solidly for two days and two nights. When I woke up I couldn't touch meat, it made me feel disgusted, and I had completely lost my anger. I felt as if a flower had opened in my heart, so much peace and understanding. The master said that he had given me his complete knowledge by direct transmission. Only now do I appreciate these things more, and many positive things have happened. When I told him that I was returning to England, and asked how he could teach me, the other disciples laughed and said that the master didn't need a telephone. The teaching would continue, and after I returned he did in fact come to me in dreams. I began to accept more and more the reality of non-physical communication.

What the Chinese call 'Above Teachers' are beings from other planes of reality, disincarnate masters, who teach us in order that we may become better people. Some of them have made a contract with us before we have come into this body, and it is their duty to guide us.

My second special teacher is a very powerful healer in Beijing. I spent time with her in a Chinese medical centre where she is actively curing people of all kind of problems. One Australian man there had some kind of stone in his gallbladder. The teacher said some words, passed her hand over him and told him to go to toilet. He urinated the stone out. She has a collection of such stones from the people she has healed.

An eighty year old lady was brought in by her two sons. She was hunchbacked and close to death. The teacher told them that she couldn't cure their mother as it was her time to die. They asked her again and again, until she agreed. She said the words 'black, black' over the old lady's head and the lady's hair turned black. She dragged her fingers up and down her spine, did something with her hands and the old lady's spine straightened up.

The more people my teacher heals the stronger she becomes. Healing is a two sided activity. After a year or so of healing I began to realise the nature and purpose of disease. It is very much related to the law of karma, to the universal laws. My first teacher would only heal someone if they specifically asked him. The idea is that there is a learning to be had from the disease, and if it is just taken away from you then you will not absorb the lesson.

You need good mental capacity when you study chi-gung. As a human you will want to explain the strange things that will happen to you. One way to nourish the brain and the intellect is to absorb the energy from the jing, or sexual essence, directly into the brain. If you do chi gung incorrectly you can go mad. In China I often saw people out in open spaces talking to trees, and there was a woman who would laugh at the moon. My teacher said she had done incorrect chi gung practice.

Because we are still human, we should do things that are not too far from our reality. Sometimes you will go to places that have no time or

space. Distant-healers do this but often don't realise. My third special teacher has gone beyond physicality and is not limited by his body. He can call the dragon from the sky and ride to heaven on it's back. He can pass through material objects. When people hear these things they think it is impossible, but there is more to existence than people can imagine.

Martial arts is my life, and for me it is a struggle against the self and not against other people. If you have to test your skills it is because you lack faith in yourself. If you must test them then do so against muggers and against injustice. The karmic effect will not be so severe. Martial arts is an excellent path to find spirituality. So many people come close to opening up, to finding a higher level of being, but they don't allow themselves to do it. They should cultivate their intuition and follow it. Ultimately if we evolve we will leave this plane of existence and enter other dimensions where totally different laws apply.

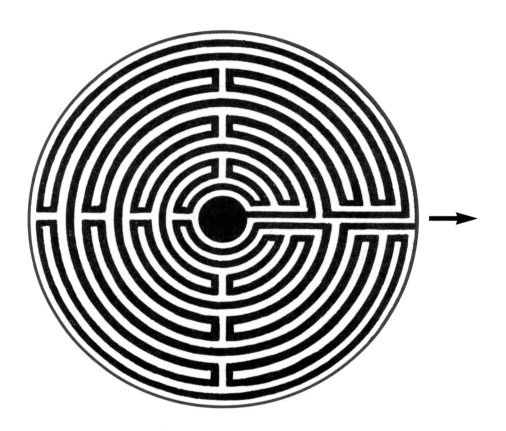

Chapter Nine

Through The Mists Of The Sacred Mountains... And Beyond...

When I first travelled to the Far East as a seventeen year old boy, I was fascinated by the internal martial arts and eager to find a master who could guide me into the very depths of both the physical and the spiritual aspects of practice. On my return to Europe I continued to seek out teachers of various esoteric traditions, and more often than not they appeared when I least expected. Shivanath is one such man, and someone who would even deny being a teacher in any formal sense of the word.

Shivanath with his bow.

Having spent ten years living in a monastery as a Hindu priest, and a lifetime spent researching mystical systems from both the East and the West, Shivanath is a man who seems to have stepped out of another age. Naturally humble and intelligent by nature I was initially drawn to his company by the stream of deep insights which emerged from him as he went about his daily life. In the following years we went on to share both knowledge and friendship, as well as a teacher in the form of Dr. Serge Augier. Living a quiet life in a small village on the Welsh coast, Shivanath has a special interest in the warrior-skill of crafting weapons in the old way, using mystical knowledge - which has all but vanished in our society - to imbue the knives, bows and arrows with a potent energy. He sees all of his various skills - from rune reading, to chanting ancient Vedic mantras, to martial arts - as tools which help him on his unique journey back to the Source, back to Krishna.

Before my most recent trip to the Far East, when I would be visiting the sacred mountains of China, I travelled yet again to the mystical hills of Wales to glean some knowledge which I hoped would make my forthcoming journey even more fruitful. Here are some of the teachings I absorbed from Shivanath.

The Path Of The Mystic Warrior

The mystic warrior lives in a world of subtle powers, and his way is to rely on these powers no matter what. These powers are connected to intuition. Most people in today's society are intellect personified, and their intuition is dormant. That is why they rely on their shoulders and arms, which are manipulative energies, rather than on their centres, which are intuitive. When you contact the subtle bodies, the power bodies, you begin to get mystic powers which don't follow the ways of this world. Then you are able to do things which cannot be explained. In this society we are taught to be walking machines, in fact we are disempowered at every step. The internal martial arts can help you to contact your subtle energies, and then you have unlimited power. Fighting is just one expression of that

The will resides in the belly, and it is the will that really achieves anything. Actions are secondary to will. A mystic accomplishes what needs to be done without physically doing anything. Ancient warriors would constantly train their power and subtle energy rather than their technique. They would pit their power against each other in feats that today would be dismissed as magic or myth. The Vedic scriptures are full of such stories. Warriors such as Arjuna or Hanuman were so linked up to the universal powers that they could kill an enemy by speaking a mantra. Equally they could heal someone in the same way. Also, if you have enough power you will naturally avoid danger.

When a mystic martial artist made a weapon it would be done in a sacred way. Such a warrior or craftsman would know that a weapon is a being, not an object. Your life and the life of the weapon become intertwined as one, and it might take years in the making. Such a weapon would be handed down through the generations, from father to son or from master to disciple. A weapon could never be used by anyone but it's owner, although it could be transferred with a ritual. A warrior may even find a weapon, if his destiny was entwined with it, or he could be led to it by a dream or a deva (a bright being or an angel).

The material for the weapon must come from the right place that contains just the energy you need. The time that the crafting begins must be astrologically correct, and you would even work on it only on certain days in order that only specific energies went into the weapon. Also the place where it is made and the consciousness of the craftsman are important factors. Once it is made the weapon will be installed by it's owner, which means that a certain spirit will come and inhabit it. The user must be able to merge his mind with the spirit of the weapon to become one with it, and after he must care for it so that the energy doesn't dissipate. It's making can be empowered by the use of mantras, runes or yantras (sacred shapes which harness energy) made from certain stones. As you can see, this whole process is a far cry from just putting a piece of wood or metal in a machine and turning it into a staff or a knife.

Runes or sacred words play a role in mystical martial traditions in the east and the west. The Nordic runes are interesting in that each one, if used correctly, manifests one of the energies which make up the physical universe. On the bow that I made recently, for example, I carved the following runes :

SOWELA - this is raw power without any specific direction.

TAWOZ - represents fire energy and determination and keeps the arrow on a straight line.

DAGAZ - this is the rune of the self and it gives the power to go inwards and meditate. It centres the consciousness, for if you centre the mind the arrow will hit the centre of the target. Remember that in archery the arrow follows the mind.

One of the big problems nowadays is that people have lost touch with nature and with themselves. Practices such as the internal martial arts and meditation can lead you back towards the source, into the subtle aspects of your self and back to where the real power lies. The true warrior would rather die than sell out or disempower himself, in the knowledge that material gain is a fleeting illusion, whereas mystical power gained through spiritual power will stay with one for lifetime after lifetime.

To The Peak Of Omei Shan

Huge crowds of people everywhere; the smells of Chinese food; awesome landscape scenery interspersed with dirty, polluted cities the likes of which can be seen in every country; and the thrill of being in China, heading towards the western province of Szechuan where I would begin my climb up Omei Shan, a mountain sacred to the Buddhists and famed as a centre of traditional boxing.

As my train neared the end of it's thirty six hour journey from Guangzhou, I peered out at the rolling hills and wondered if I would see any Omei boxing, or even if I would recognise it as something apart from the modernised wushu forms that could be seen being practised everywhere in China. It was a few more hours bus ride from the city of Chengdu before I reached Omei Village, a quiet and attractive little place which sits right at the foot of the mountain, and almost at once I came across picturesque Bao Guo Monastery which was said to be several hundred years old.

It was there I met Master Zhang Ya Kui, eighth generation inheritor of the Green Tree Omei Boxing system and a teacher of Hsing-I Chuan and Tai Chi. He told me that the Omei boxing systems, of which there were many branches, originated several hundred years ago when people frequently travelled through Szechuan on their way to and from the west. Adepts of northern and southern systems exchanged knowledge, giving rise to methods which contained a balanced blend of long and short range fighting techniques. The Green Tea system has static chi-gung as it's central practice, with the aim being to make the body very strong inside and out. There were several forms for both solo and partner training, and routines for long staff and short stick. Master Zhang told me that his older boxing brother was famous for being able to do a handstand on two fingers of one hand, and explained that this kind of ability is only possible if the adept has remarkable control over his internal power. I saw a photo of the man's two-finger feat, and although I have yet to see it in person I am sure that such a thing is possible. Certainly it is indicative of exceptional strength and balance.

I began climbing the mountain before dawn the next day, happily following three Tibetan Buddhist pilgrims for an hour before realising that they had strayed from the main path and were now completely disorientated. An hour later I rejoined the path, and covered in mud from the various small ravines that I and my new friends had inevitably slipped down I decided to follow my intuition this time. The path was fairly steep, with a quiet flow of pilgrims chanting mantras on their beads, and every hour or so a ramshackle shop or a small row of food stalls. At each of these places I saw wooden walking sticks hanging from racks, and often had one thrust into my hand by a shopkeeper hoping I would buy his wares. What did I want with a walking stick? I thought to myself each time it happened. A few hours later I was to find out just why so many pilgrims on Omei Shan did carry sticks.

Once my teacher Serge Augier told me of the time he spent with some full-grown tigers in a circus in Paris. The tigers were obviously kept in secure cages, but the keepers warned Serge not to go near the bars. One man, they told him, had put the lens of his camera through the bars when the tiger had been resting at the far end of the cage, some twenty feet away. He was happily shooting away when there was a blur and the tiger bit his arm. Ever so slowly the creature pulled the man through the bars as everyone looked on helplessly. Watching those awesome creatures for several days, Serge came to the conclusion that he could barely imagine someone defeating a fully-grown tiger. We had heard stories, of course, of Indonesian Pentjak Silat masters going into the jungle and killing tigers, and of a karate master who put himself in a cage armed with a pair of sai against a half-starved tiger and winning the match. Later that night, as I sat in a quiet monastery courtyard overlooking the stunning scenery of Omei Shan, I thought about all these things and wondered.

Mankind may seem puny and helpless against many of the other creatures in nature, but our real strength lays in our ability to contact the deepest and most subtle energies of the universe, to become self-realised. There are many stories about such self-realised men interacting with fearsome creatures without any violence being done. The Chinese Buddhist monk Xu Yun (Empty Cloud), who died in the latter half of this century at the grand age of a hundred and twenty, spent his whole life wandering the mountains of China and living in the wilderness.

Once a tiger entered the meditation hall where he was teaching, and all the monks ran away in panic. Xu Yun gave the Buddhist prayer of refuge to the animal, who became docile and seemed to listen to the teaching. Another Buddhist monk, the renowned Phra Acharn Mun of Thailand, spent most of his life living in the deep jungles which were home to countless tigers. Often he would sit in meditation in the mouth of a cave that was on a path used every day by a certain tiger. He related to his disciples how he would emanate loving compassion to all creatures, and he was never attacked by any animals. If one of the monks showed signs of fear, he would instruct them to meditate in an area of forest that teemed with tigers, and there are no records of any of them being eaten. The sixteenth century Indian saint Chaitanya Mahaprabhu, whom Indians consider to be an incarnation of Lord Krishna, once walked through the jungle singing his praises to the Lord with such devotion that the trees and the animals, including tigers and elephants, began dancing along with him

Mid-afternoon, and the sweat was pouring from me as I walked steadily up a stone path that was sheer cliff on one side and a thousand foot drop, ending in deep forest, on the other. I had seen no other travellers for an hour or so, only a trail of droppings on the track that indicated to me that the infamous monkeys had been around. They must be interesting creatures to meet, I thought to myself, just before several of them came dropping from the trees above me and began leaping around on the ground. I put up both palms to show I had nothing to give them, and after a minute or two they left. So that is what they are like, I thought with a smile, just before I saw something way ahead on the path that was far too big to be a monkey.

No, it can't be a monkey, I reassured myself, it must be a man walking down the path towards me, even if he is walking like a King travelling through his territory. Closer and closer it came until, yes, by the gods, it must be the mother and father of all monkeys, it was huge, and it wasn't in the least bit phased by open palms or hand clapping. It came directly

up to me and pulled off my woolly hat, it's primordial red eyes full of violence as it hissed angrily, baring it's sharp teeth so that the hairs on my body stood on end. It reached into my pockets looking for food and as I patted it's arms down it hissed even louder. Time stood still as I inwardly chanted a mantra to Hanuman, the monkey God who protects the devotees of God, praying with all my heart . "Aiiyee, Aiiyee!" came the call, as an old man ran down the track waving a stick at the monkey. The creature hissed one last time and leaped into the trees. I wiped the sweat from my brow and wondered what would have happened if...

A short while later I had something akin to an answer, for I saw the same huge monkey. fighting another one, and it's movement showed that it was a master fighter, loose, very fast, spontaneous, agile, completely unpredictable, and with a power that rattled the other creatures body. More than those qualities was it's spirit. It fought to the utmost to survive with a mind made strong through eons of living on the mountains. To defeat such a creature would take amazing skill.

I contemplated these various men and their lives, and then began doing my Tai Chi form beneath the stars, natures most beautiful blanket. Half way through the form I became aware of something shining down the mountain, and glancing upwards I saw a shaft of bright light coming from the sky. There were no aircraft in sight, just a sky full of stars and the beautiful, subtle light. My spirit soared with the wonder of it, and I completed the form and sat still beneath something I could not explain. Early the next morning, as I approached the peak of Omei Shan, a Chinese pilgrim approached me and told me in clear English, "If we are lucky today, we may see the Buddha Light!" I smiled and nodded, and gave a silent prayer that every being might have the same aspiration.

To The Peak Of Wutang Shan

Wu Tang Shan has a special place in the annals of Chinese martial arts legend, and sits alongside the Shaolin monastery as one of the two major sites of boxing development. Shaolin martial arts, of course, are heavily influenced by Buddhist thought and practice, whereas Wu Tang boxing flourished in the stream of Taoist philosophy which has flowed for thousands of years in China. Situated in the northwest of Hubei Province, the Wu Tang mountains actually cover an area of several hundred kilometres with seventy two major peaks, the major one being some 4000 metres tall. Here, amidst scenery so beautiful that it really must make the Gods smile, the Taoist priest Chang Sanfeng is said to have received the art of Tai Chi Chuan in a dream. Could he have guessed I wondered, as I rumbled along a dusty road in the back of a van laden with people, sacks of rice and building materials, that several hundred years later many Westerners would make it their dream to visit this scared site and practice Tai Chi Chuan in it's timeless atmosphere?

Hunched in between two grinning young men I eagerly awaited the opportunity. After a couple of hours I heard the driver call out "Wu Tang" and before I could jump out to freedom a bearded man wearing the beard and hairstyle of a Taoist monk - and a new Adidas tracksuit - jumped in the van and in rapid-fire fashion began reeling off the names of various Chinese internal martial art styles - "Tai Chi, Ba Gua Chang, Hsing-I Chuan!" I nodded speechlessly and he led me out onto the street in busy Wu Tang Village and down a series of back alleys, past pigs and children playing in dirt, until we reached a large open space surrounded on three sides by single story rooms and on the forth by a river.

This was the school of Master Li Chiao Fu, the young monk who had greeted me quite inexplicably - no one knew of me or my arrival in Wu Tang - and the fourteenth generation head of the Wu Tang Chuan system. Raised as a boy in the famous Shaolin monastery before becoming a Taoist monk in the temples of Wu Tang Shan, Li has spent his whole life practising the internal martial arts, and it shows in his boundless energy, his happy and natural demeanour, and the swiftness and power of his forms. His school is typical of boxing academies in China : the students, ranging from five years of age to twenty five, practice four times a day for two hours each time starting at five in the morning. After graduation they return to their home towns where they can become teachers in their own right. Master Li emphasises endless repetition of the basic stances, footwork and strikes, both as forms and on bags, and also considers standing-post chi-gung to be a vital element of daily practice. I stayed at the school for a week and began learning the first form of Wu Tang Chuan, which begins like a mixture of Hsing-I and Tai Chi and then moves into Ba Gua type techniques. The system contains four hand forms, and sets for the sword and other weapons, as well as Taoist meditation and chi-gung methods

On the last day of my stay Master Li guided me up Wu Tang Shan, a steep climb which takes several hours through alternately thick mist and

Master Li - Bagua Heaven Palms.

stunning mountain scenery. At the peak is an ancient monastic complex, and here Li pointed out the various places he had stayed as a young monk. He stopped me at the top of a stone staircase and asked me to pick up a long, iron sword which sat in a rack slightly beneath us. I tried and tried but I could not lift it an inch. Li smiled and told me that he would watch his old master practice with that sword faster than most men could wield one of normal weight. Later, in a temple courtyard halfway down the mountain, I saw circles worn into the stone where men had walked the Ba Gua circle over the generations. The Ba Gua Chang styles on Wu Tang Shan, claimed Li, far predated the style of the famous Dong Hai Chuan, and having seen them I feel that they certainly have a flavour all their own.

Master Li with Bagua application.

It was a special moment for me sitting beside a cheerful Taoist monk on the peak of that sacred mountain, staring into the void of the thick clouds and letting my mind wander back through the mists of time to a story told to me by one of my first teachers. It was set in an age when anything was possible

They faced each other across the empty courtyard, far beneath the circling gaze of the grey carrion birds who eagerly awaited their next meal. This was the moment that the leaders of the sects had been contemplating these past long years, the final confrontation which would decide once and for all the final resting place of the Kahl.

Mang eyed his enemy and felt nothing but hatred. The man-boy facing him was a living example of the detested morals of the Taoist sect. Mang despised and secretly feared the hypocritical, paradoxical views of the warrior-monks, who trained in the most ancient arts of destruction and yet were avowed not to take life in any event. The enemy faced him coolly, showing no sign of fear or hatred but simply a look of acceptance, like one who knew that this was his place for good or bad

Shub began his first level breathing exercise. Fear, his ever-present companion, was making it's presence felt particularly strongly in this

encounter, but he accepted that as the inevitable result of the long build-up to this day and he allowed himself to analyse his feelings without becoming overpowered by them.

The two approached each other across the desolate arena which had been set aside for this very moment. A high stone wall surrounded the earthen floor, with a single archway being the only way in or out. As they drew within the long range each became aware of subtle nuances of character given away by breath, posture and gait. Each knew that the other would read instantly any weakness and be aware of any flaw should one falter for even an instant. They stopped just short of the medium range, Mang immediately adopting the favoured posture of his sect. Mimicking the great black tiger of the southern plains, his knees were well bent, hands in front of the body, the fingers curled into the semblance of claws. Mang knew well the power of his claw-hands, having seen many an opponent fall dead as their power tore through the soft tissue of the throat. His whole body tensed as he waited for his enemy to adopt a fighting stance. The Taoists had many fighting forms at their disposal, and Mang had gone to great pains the learn the weak points of each one. He was leaving nothing to chance in this encounter for more than just his life depended on it.

Instead of assuming a classical posture the enemy simply stood quietly, seemingly totally relaxed and unlike one preparing to do battle to the death. Mang waited, fearing a trick, a bead of sweat running down his forehead and into his eye. He cursed himself. How had he allowed his attention to be consumed by something as unimportant as his own sweat? He refocused on his opponent and mentally rechecked every aspect of the other's posture. It seemed that the enemy was simply unprepared for the coming battle and had decided to accept death without a struggle. So be it. He prepared himself for the moment when he would strike out, adding to his list of victims and ending the boy's short life.

Shub watched with interest as his opponent proceeded to get hotter and hotter under the ferocious sun. All that tension must be terribly painful, he mused. He had not seen the fighting systems of the Lings before and was suprised at how much they differed from his own. After all, had his own master not taught him that all the sects were part of one family? He wondered at how such differences could arise between the methods employed by the schools. He had heard about the so-called external

Master Li instructs the author in Wudang Boxing.

fighting styles, of course, and suddenly he had an insight into what that term meant. The man before him was mimicking the outward, or external, movements of a tiger, that was obvious, but it was very different from the Taoists who sought to use the spirit and energy of certain creatures, or to learn lessons from their behaviour.

Mang noticed the enemy's attention wander for just an instant and he took the opportunity to strike. He leaped forward, stamping with his foot in an attempt to crush the bones in the boy's left leg. Simultaneously he thrust his hand at the boy's throat in a tearing motion that would be the last thing the boy felt.

Instead of the crack of bones and the satisfying feeling of warm blood on his fingers, Mang felt nothing. It was as if the enemy had simply vanished. He span around to see the boy still standing in the same nonchalant posture some distance away. Enraged by his lack of success Mang charged forward again, this time sending one hand to the boy's throat and the other to his groin. Once again the result was the same. The boy simply seemed to disappear in front of his eyes. Now Mang realised that the basic techniques and awesome strength which had sufficed to defeat all-comers up until that point were no match for the black-robed youngster he faced in that arena. He began to worry, his concern obviously showing as a broad smile appeared on his opponent's face. Only one thing was left to do. His teachers had shown him a method, one which they said he must never use unless his life was in danger.

He forced his fears down into the pit of his stomach and poured his focus onto them until they were transformed into a ball of fury which he projected into his right hand.

Shub was feeling very pleased with himself as he watched the sweat streaming down the bare chest of his opponent. He smiled inwardly at the ease with which he had evaded the furious rush of the huge, bald-headed young man. He was still smiling when the blow caught him, Mang's hand shooting out with such speed that both of them were stunned. The hand seemed to glow with a reddish light and Mang could feel it pulsating madly as it hit the boy's body. Not the best of targets, but the boy would never forget that blow. He backed away to observe the damage he had done.

Shub was staggered by the blow which he had neither seen nor felt coming. He had been warned countless times about becoming smug and had fallen into the trap which he had tried so hard to avoid. His ribs were ablaze with pain and his whole side threatened to seize up. Automatically he began the fourth level breathing pattern, his mind instantly relieved from the pain in his side. He saw that his opponent had back away a little to gloat over his success and he thanked the heavens that the attack had not continued with equal fury. In a few moments he had composed himself, but what he saw next almost drove him to his knees with despair.

Mang had found it. Quite by chance he had discovered the greatest secret of his sect, thought to be lost to all but a few long-dead masters who had jealously guarded it's methods. Looking down at his hands he saw a globe of red light pulsating in his hand. So, he thought, this is the true meaning of the fabled Great Red Fist. He had heard many explanations of the term in the past, but now he really knew for himself! He fondled the ball of energy in his hands with great joy. It had a feeling of solidity about it which Mang was at a loss to explain. Having lusted over his new-found power for a few moments he turned his gaze back to his enemy, just in time to see the look of despair on the boy's face.

Shub had heard tales of the Great Red Fist. It was a method developed by some twisted warrior many generations back. Legend had it that once in control of his inner power, he could create a weapon of energy which could be launched at will. This was one weapon which Shub had wished many times he would never have to face, and now it was to be his doom.

Mang was astonished at the power he now held, with some difficulty, between his shaking hands. The force of the globe seemed to be increasing all the time, making him hold on ever more strongly, yet the stronger he held on the more force it contained. Then a realisation hit him and he squeezed every bit of his strength down onto the glowing orb of destruction, which responded by doubling in size and glowing and pulsating with more force and fury than ever before. At the last

Master Li with a Taoist brother and the author.

moment, just when he was sure he could hold on no longer, Mang hurled the globe at his enemy, concentrating it's potency at the boy's chest.

Gripped by a panic worse than he had ever felt before Shub had no time for thought as the fireball raced across the small gap towards him. An instant later his body was thrown to the ground. A fierce burning raged through him, scorching his flesh and burning his head. He was completely paralysed by the blast, unable to breathe or think. He lay awaiting the final blow which would send him to the other side.

Several minutes passed. Somehow Shub gathered enough strength to raise his head and look towards his opponent. Mang lay sprawled on the earth in a posture similar to his own, totally motionless. Shub slowly hauled himself to his feet and half staggered and half fell towards the crumpled figure. A vague motion of the chest showed that the man still clung to life, however feebly. Standing over him Shub realised that there was one final task to perform. He must finish the battle which had raged on through the generations by delivering the final blow and killing his opponent. The very thought sickened him. It was one thing to kill a warrior who was trying to kill him, but quite another matter to end the life of a man who lay helpless in front of him. What of the vow he had taken in front of the Abbot, that he would never take a life? But then why had the masters of his order sent him here, to this arena, where death and victory were inseparable? A small movement in his opponent's body warned him that he didn't have much time in which to decide. Strike or hold back? The decision rested firmly on his shoulders. His master was no longer with him.

Mang's head was a confusion of blurred images accompanied by a cacophonous percussion which threatened to burst his ear drums. He had been aware of the moment of victory as the raging fireball drove into the boy, sending him to his doom. But a moment later the joy had turned sour when it became clear that the boy had not been totally destroyed. At that point Mang had felt all the strength leave his body and he crumpled uselessly to the ground. Although aware of everything around him he was unable to move so much as a little finger. It was clear that the Great Red Fist had stolen all of his strength. So that was why it had died out so long ago! Oh what a foolish weapon, he thought helplessly. There was the barest amount of life force in him, just enough to keep him alive. He wondered how long he would have to lie there before his strength returned. Then he saw, to his horror, the boy stumbling towards him. So, he had survived the Great Red Fist! By the gods, was he human or immortal? So this would be it. There was no feeling of hatred left, no cursing himself for his inexcusable failure, just a calm acceptance of the inevitable. His head rolled to the side and he awaited the brief moment of pain which would signal his exit from this world.

An instant of fear was replaced by incredulity as Mang realised that the palm extended towards his chest was shimmering with the silvery glow often associated with the great healing masters of the various sects. He felt a warm glow enter his body and immediately strength began to move through him, revitalising every part of his being.

"Shub. " The boy offered his name.

"I am... Mang. " The two exchanged brief eye contact before Shub turned and limped sorely across the arena. He stopped at the tall archway which had been built into the stone wall. On the ground beneath it was a wooden table. A purple cushion rested on the table, and on the cushion squatted a fist-sized crystal of pure black obsidian, a perfect orb which virtually hummed with contained power and subtle energy. Now the Kahl, that most prized of sacred objects, would find rest in a secluded Taoist monastery. Shub reached down and picked up the crystal, and as he did so he was filled with a joyous energy. Without a backward glance he left the arena and headed north. But it was not to be the last time that he and the huge warrior named Mang were to meet...

I opened my eyes to see Master Li swooping down into a low, extended posture as he performed his Ba Gua form before a crowd of curious onlookers, and I thought about the value of such stories and of how they had been used down through the ages as tools to deliver insights to the student. Later, as we descended from the peak of Wu Tang Shan, I remembered the teachings I had learned from various Taoists over the past fifteen years.

Taoism is a gift from the Universe by which we can understand it's energies. It teaches us through poetry, whispers, shadows, for the Tao is forever elusive but ever-present, incapable of being known by the intellect but easily appreciated by the childlike heart of the sage. Modern man seeks to dominate nature, to control everything he sees, to build walls of logic and conceptual understanding around his life. The sage lets go of these things and cultivates intuition, feeling, imagination and the subtle energies. He sees his questions answered in the shape of clouds in the sky, in the patterns of fallen twigs, in dreams and visions, and he rides the wave of chi which permeates all of creation with a joyousness that makes life truly worth living.

As I bowed goodbye to Master Li, and saw how joyful and centred he was in the midst of the most basic of living conditions, I realised yet again the value of these internal arts that we practice. I had given Sifu Li a walkman tapeplayer, and my final memory of Wu Tang village was of a happy, bearded Taoist monk, clad in a shiny Adidas tracksuit, bobbing his head up and down to the beat of music as he waved me goodbye. Onwards, then, to Hong.

The Hsing-I Masters Of Hong Kong

I made my way through the towering skyscrapers of Hong Kong island having arrived from China by coach. Each time I go to that city it seems to have sprouted a dozen new buildings, and invariably I go to one of it's many parks to practice by myself or to study with a teacher. On my last visit to Hong Kong I had met with my teacher Paul Whitrod who opened up the doors for me to meet several highly respected internal martial artists. Previous to that I had met David Hun, a teacher of I-Chuan, whose own practice was based on simplicity, minimilistic training methods and the cultivation of energy and whole-body power. I-Chuan, which has recently been gaining popularity in the West, is a very interesting system in that it distils the essence of the internal martial arts into a few exercises and drills, eschewing long forms in favour of energy work much in the same way as does Tzuranmen. When I first saw Sifu Hun he was holding the standing-post chi-gung posture for over an hour, his body very still and his eyes fixed on some distant point. Later he gave me instruction for that exercise.

"Keep the weight forward on the balls of the feet. Wrap the fascia around the bones of the arms and legs in a spiralic fashion. Always direct your gaze forward. Put your intent down into the earth and simultaneously up to heaven, The arms are sung (loose), the legs are bound. The fingers spread open whilst keeping soft, and you visualise a sphere of energy between your palms. "

It was simple advice, but the effects of the exercise were many and quite profound. Later the posture can be changed to many variations so that it becomes more of a fighting-stance, and the next stage is to begin pulsing energy through the body.

Another interesting teacher was Sifu Tss- st (earting). Sifu Tang said that his art was the original style of Hsing-I Chuan, and it was indeed quite different to the commonly seen styles. His pi-chuan (splitting fist) was a strike with the shoulder, head and arm, cutting all the way down.

Beng Chuan (crushing fist) used the dan-tien or belly to strike the opponent, whereas Pao Chuan (pounding fist) hit with the chest, and used a closing and opening of the scapula and back to release power. Tsuan (drilling fist) was very slippery and water-like, evading and striking in a snake-like manner. Heng (crossing fist) drew energy inwards, for defending and striking. The forms of Sifu Tang's system were based on ten animals, and in each posture the six-harmonies were manifest and the eyes stared forward. What most impressed me about this teacher was his use of the dan-tien to release power ; it was very clear when he did his forms that energy was coming from his belly, up his spine, and out of his striking hand or arm. He explained to me that the whole system was based upon the movement of five circles within the body, creating a sphere which could produce power in any direction at will.

My final port of call in Hong Kong was to a certain Sifu Chang , a master of Tai Chi, Ba Gua and Hsing-I who had trained under several renowned masters in Shanghai. More than fifty years old and blind in one eye, Sifu Chang gave me a startling lesson one night in his small flat in the outer reaches of the New Territories. Lightly holding my arms he said, "This is the energy of Pi-Chuan", and then without any discernable physical movement I felt a current of energy run through my body and down into my feet. He repeated the process with each of the five elemental energies of Hsing-I, as all the while his one good eye sparkled with sprit. I was shocked. It was the first time I had felt such a thing being done to me on a purely energetic level, without any gross physical movement. On his cue I then sent a punch at the Sifu's head, only to found myself bouncing off of the wall without feeling him touch me or knowing what he had just done.

He was really at a high level of practice, and later that night he told me that in his opinion few people really understood the concepts of the internal arts, and fewer could use energy and power in combat without large physical movements. Teachers of various internal arts with over twenty years experience had come to him and received the same lesson, and always he told them that if they wished to study with him they must give up their present practice and start over from the beginning. Few of them wished to do such a thing, of course, and so Sifu Chang taught just a handful of dedicated students. The advice he gave me was useful. Go deeply into one internal style and you will find the energy of them all. Use the mind, not the muscle. The concept of Sung means to make your movements soft and relaxed but very alive and alert. And finally make your movements smaller and smaller until there is no external movement, only the movement of energy.

Tai Chi Master Chen Yun San

Back in Taiwan the following month I continued my training with Sifu Chen Yun San in a small park in the north of Taipai. A cheerful, bright eyed man whose movement belies his fifty years of age, Sifu Chen has practiced martial arts for most of his life under several great masters, beginning at the age of four with his grandfather who was a renowned internal boxer and doctor. He is also an experienced Buddhist adept having trained under the famous Master Nan Huai Chin and other Tibetan Buddhist Grandmasters. When I first saw him walking in the park I talked my Chinese friends into asking him what he did, for his gait looked so balanced and smooth that I instinctively knew he must have been doing some kind of practice.

My intuition was confirmed a short time later when he took his jacket off and began moving through a Tai Chi form with great fluidity and latent power, It turned out that Sifu Chen had been the bodyguard to the son of Taiwan's President, was the teacher of the guards of government officials, and was highly respected as a healer having helped bring people back to health who had been given up on by the local hospital. His father had been a doctor of Chinese medicine, and his approach to his practice was so gentle (most of the students in his early morning class were middle-aged people interested in keeping healthy) that I wondered just how skilled a martial artist he was. The first time we touched arms I found out. It was as if his whole body had eyes, and his movement was so smooth and loose that every time I attacked it was like falling into water and then being suddenly repulsed. He had the same broken-rhythm, deceptive footwork that I had seen previously being used by Serge Augier, although I had not seen it demonstrated by other teachers of Tai Chi. It was that footwork that seemed to make a lot of the Tai Chi movements really work well, and I wondered if certain teachers kept that hidden from their students or if it had been lost due to the emphasis on form and pushing hands.

At out first meeting Sifu Chen held my left hand for a long time as he continued talking about his practice. My hand was cold, he said, which indicated that I had been doing too much hard practice. I admitted that he was right; in fact for a couple of months I had been working intensely on certain hard chi-gung practices which had resulted in increased body strength but also some uncomfortable sensations. He continued by saying that the practice had damaged my liver. My palms were yellow and cold, my fingertips pink, indicating that energy was reaching the tips but it was not of a strong quality. If I agreed to stop the hard practice he would teach me, he said, and when he put my hand down it was full of warmth and energy. I felt his own hands : they were as soft as a baby's and very warm. I happily began taking lessons from him each morning in the calm atmosphere of an earthen area surrounded by beautiful old trees. He gave me various exercises from the internal arts which he said would complement what I was already doing. From Ba Gua he showed me how to walk around a tree, drawing energy in

Chen Yun San with author doing Tai Chi Form.

through the palms as they pointed towards the trunk. After an hour or so of this I felt a noticeable effect - increased energy in the body, an openness in the chest and a new connectedness to the earth. Every three days I would move to a new tree, for the leaves would turn yellow and , according to my teacher, the tree would be in danger of dying. He helped me also to find a deeper degree of relaxation and looseness in my Tai Chi form, telling me that Tai Chi is a moving meditation whose core idea was to relax deeply and to be aware of the points of balance and yin and yang within each posture. Every movement in life should be Tai Chi, with complete awareness and a relaxed but alert mind and body. He made me do the postures slower than I had ever done them before, and what resulted was a far deeper sense of harmony and body awareness.

During training one morning, Sifu Chen lightly brushed my chest as if flicking away a speck of dust to demonstrate to some students the soft hand of Tai Ch. Several hours later I began to feel the effects of the seemingly light strike. Headache, heart palpitations and the feeling that my blood pressure had risen, were some of the symptoms. I had difficulty in sleeping during the following two nights. I spent my time lying in bed feeling that I was just about to leave this world. When I returned to see my teacher, he was very apologetic and explained that he had accidentally released a burst of internal energy. He cured me with some simple chi kung and massage. I was truly impressed by the damage that such a light strike could cause.

For me Sifu Chen epitomises the ideal of a Tai Chi master : a gentleman, a skilled fighter, and a joyous human being with a deep understanding of how spiritual practice and martial arts are related.

Of Bagua And White Crane

One night at Eric Lo's Ba Gua class I met an interesting student of his named Shih Kuo-Ping, a bright-eyed Chan Buddhist monk who had been born and raised in Czechoslovakia before spending the past five years in a Taiwanese Buddhist monastery. Kuo-Ping knew several skilled masters in Taipai, and kindly introduced me to a couple of them.

Imagine my surprise when he told me he had been studying with Master Her Shun Ting, whom I had been trying to locate since my arrival in that country. Her was the teacher of my first Ba Gua instructor, Michael

Chen Yun San appying Tai Chi movements to the author.

Gillespie, who had laid my foundation in the internal arts. A former Major-General in the Taiwanese Airforce, Her was respected in Taiwan as the inheritor of Sun Lu-Tang's Ba Gua Chang. I met him early one morning as he gave a class to a small group of students in a downtown Taipai park, and watching him I was very impressed that a man in his eighties was walking the circle with such agility and lightness. An intelligent man with a ready smile and alert eyes, Master Her apologised for being too old to show me the usage of the internal arts. Then he hit me with Hsing-I's beng chuan (crushing fist) from two inches away, and I went back with the force of the strike. He had juice, that old man. He explained that the crucial point in practice was to develop energy in the dan-tien through internal breathing methods. A young man, he said, should train very hard and engage in fighting skills to understand what he is doing. In middle age one should move more into chi-gung practice, and in old age one should take it easier, exercise each morning and enjoy life, not worrying about anything. I could see from the joyful look on his face that he practised what he taught.

Master Chen showing Tai Chi application for a throw.

Later, Kuo-Ping took me to meet his White-Crane boxing master, who was named Lin, and I watched his students repeating seemingly simple drills for an hour at a time. Typical of Southern White Crane boxing were the short, whipping hand techniques, high narrow stances and the emphasis on explosive power. A senior student showed a form done at very high speed, and then asked if I would like to push hands with him. His upper body was very strong and I reverted to a softer, more yielding approach to deal with his attacks. We had a few fast, spirited exchanges and then I was shown a video of Master Lin doing various feats of chi-gung. One included him lifting a child in a basket using only his ear!

Another showed him breaking two steel spears on his eyelids! Like many southern Chinese arts, these White-Crane boxers really took body conditioning to its limits.

Conclusion

My journey through the world of the esoteric and internal martial arts has been rewarding and exciting, and has enabled me to meet and study with a number of fascinating individuals whose work is having a positive effect on the world around them. Some of the stories you have read in this book may have been inspirational or helpful for your own practice, whilst others may seem too far-fetched to accept.

My feeling is that most human beings seriously under-use the powers given to us, including the powers of mind and energy. In ancient times, when people would dedicate whole lifetimes to mastery of the life-force which is our natural birthright, skills such as telepathy and long distance ance healing may have been much more common. Now, many people jeer at the mention of such things, but why?

Who can tell what the limits of our mind-body really are....

I wish you well in your practice, and thank you for reading this book. I am presently working on a second book on the subject, and I am happy to hear from anyone who wishes to correspond with me. Please write care of the publishers and enclose an international reply coupon with your letter.

Appendix of more photos from the author's travels

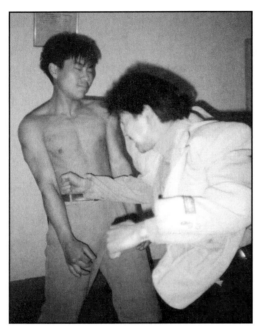

Hard chi kung Omei boxers.

Author in Taiwan in the Chiang Kai Shek memorial gardens.

*Master Lin, Southern White Crane, breaks spears
with the tips resting on his eye sockets.*

*Master Cheong demonstrates application of Phoenix
Eye Fist.*

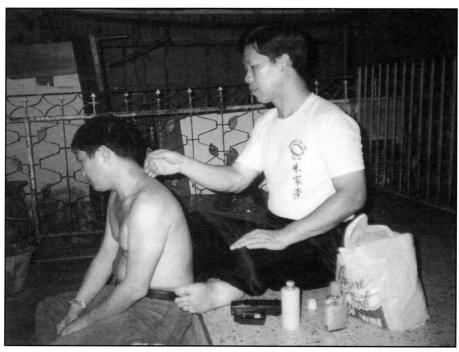

Master Cheong applying his healing hands to a patient.

Simon Das with a posture of classical Pentjak Silat.

Master Her Shun Ting

Books published by Paul H. Crompton Ltd.

Praying Mantis Kung fu	0 901764 09 4
Pak Mei Kung fu	0 901764 19 1
Aikido: Introduction to Tomiki style	0 901764 23 X
Secret Techniques Wing Chun Kung fu vol.1	0 901764 35 3
Secret Techniques Wing Chun Kung fu vol.2	0 901764 49 3
Secret Techniques Wing Chun Kung fu vol. 3	0 901764 62 0
Breaking Power of Wing Chun	0 901764 64 7
Boxe Francaise - Savate	0 901764 74 4
Essential Taekwondo Patterns	0 901764 98 1
Essentials of Wado-ryu Karate	0 901764 96 5
Tai Chi Combat	1 874250 25 1
Roaring Silence	1 874250 30 8
Spiritual Journey of Aikido	1 874250 35 9
First Steps in Aikido	1 874250 50 2
Five Steps - Meditative Sensation Walking	1 874250 60 X
Karate Kata Training	1 874250 75 8
Path to Wing Chun - 2nd edition	1 874250 80 4
Bruce Lee Anthology - Films & Fighting	1 874250 90 1
Tai Chi For Two	1 874250 40 5
Kata and Kumite for Karate	1 874250 55 3
Kendo, Way & Sport of the Sword	1 874250 81 7
Tomiki Aikido (3 volumes in 1)	1 874250 20 0
Thai Boxing Dynamite	0 901764 75 2
Tai Chi Weapons	0 901764 57 4
Shurikendo - (Study of Shuriken)	0 901764 94 9
Iaido - Way of the Stick	0 901764 58 2
Jodo - Way of the Sword	0 901764 72 8
No Need to Die - Real Techniques Survival	0 901764 41 8
Basic Monkey Boxing	0 901764 68 X
Commando Fighting Techniques	0 901764 56 6
Tai Chi Training In China	1 874250 70 7
Techniques of the Tonfa	0 901764 45 0
Shotokan Karate Free Fighting Techniques	1 874250 06 5
Introduction to Shaolin Kung Fu	0 901764 53 1
Karate Defence & Attack	0 901764 04 3
Moving Zen (U.K. only)	0 901764 51 5
Selections from the Embossed Tea Kettle -	0 901764 76 0

Videos produced by K.O.A. VIDEO – PAL, NTSC, SECAM formats.

Tai Chi Short Form
Tai Chi Chen Style
Hsing-I
Pakua – Walking Circle Sun Style
White Crane
Jujutsu
Self Defence for Today
Essential Karate
Tai Chi for Two – Push Hands
Aikido – Tomiki Randori no Kata
Aikido – Tomiki Koryu no Kata part 1
24 Step Beijing Form – Tai Chi

Available from bookstores, martial arts stores and video outlets in the United Kingdom, North America, Australasia.

Please enclose a stamped addressed envelope or I.R.C. with enquiries.
94 Felsham Road, London, sw15 1dq England
e-mail: CROMPTONPH@aol.com

Have you read the BRUCE LEE ANTHOLOGY?

This book is unbelievably popular with martial artists and fans who lived through the Bruce Lee Kung Fu boom of the seventies and eighties.

It is a collection of articles, illustrations and updates on the hectic world of martial arts before and after Bruce Lee hit the west like an eastern typhoon. The content comes mainly from the pages of "Karate & Oriental Arts" magazine, or K.O.A., which was the first martial arts magazine to be published in Great Britain (United Kingdom).

Cass Magda writes of the book:
"At times fiercely witty, and thoughtfully penetrating, this insider of the martial arts publishing business gives an interesting account of a bygone era."

Bruce Lee shattered the complacency of traditionalists, woke up the public to the martial arts, and died at the peak of a new period of his cinematic career, leaving a legacy of Jeet Kune Do, Jun Fan, Wing Chun Do and other combinations of words to describe his exploration of martial arts.

"Bruce Lee Anthology" charts much of what happened, and has new material supplied by Larry Hartsell, James DeMile, Cass Magda, Bob Breen and others.

This book is a must for anyone interested in the controversial figure who has been described as the most important martial artist of the 20th century.

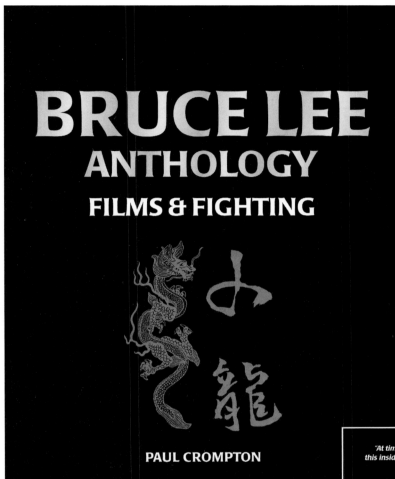

BRUCE LEE
ANTHOLOGY
FILMS & FIGHTING

PAUL CROMPTON

"At times fiercely witty, and thoughtfully penetrating, this insider of the martial art publishing business gives an interesting account of a bygone era"
CASS MAGDA

Bruce Lee struck the martial arts world like a comet from outer space. He was unexpected, devastating and original. His fans grew to millions, the world over, until now he is a legend. But what happened just before, during and after his arrival?

This Anthology is a collection of writings, illustrations, reminiscences and reflections put together by Paul Crompton, who for twenty-two years was editor of the first martial arts magazine in England, K.O.A. or "Karate & Oriental Arts".

He was in an unique position to see the panorama of martial arts, the rise of Kung Fu and the spread of the message of Jeet Kune Do, Lee's own "style" from an insider's point of view.

For many the book will be a walk down memory lane. For others it will be an eye-opener. If you are interested in martial arts, in Bruce Lee or Kung Fu, or if you are simply curious from a social point of view in what makes martial artists tick, you will find this an interesting work.

ISBN 1-874250-90-1

US $24.95

Bruce Lee Anthology - Films & Fighting
- ISBN - 1 874250 90 1